SIX GREAT VICTORIAN NOVELISTS

by

F. E. BAILY

KENNIKAT PRESS, INC.

PORT WASHINGTON, N. Y.

SIX GREAT VICTORIAN NOVELISTS

First published 1947
Reissued 1969 by Kennikat Press

Library of Congress Catalog Card No: 68-8221
Manufactured in the United States of America

FOREWORD

THE GREAT novelists whose biographies make up this book form, as it were, a little club of their own: for Thackeray knew Dickens, and Dickens was "George Eliot's" great friend, and Trollope was proposed by Thackeray for the Garrick Club, and George Meredith contributed to Dickens's magazine *All the Year Round*, and Stevenson met Meredith when he stayed at Burford Bridge.

One finds it difficult to recall any other epoch of English history when so many great novelists were writing at the same time. It was a lush period, both in literature and art.

All of these great novelists, with the exception of Meredith, died at what, nowadays, we should call an early age, though Trollope, who was sixty-seven when he died, considered himself an old man, and even when he was only fifty-five his friends reproached him for continuing to write love stories. It is no exaggeration to say that they worked themselves to death.

They were a living contradiction of the general belief that the "classic" writers wrote at great leisure solely for art's sake. They all wrote for money at the highest speed of which they were capable: Thackeray with the printer's boy waiting in the hall for copy; Trollope with his watch on the table in front of him; "George Eliot" driven on by poverty and the furious urge of female industry; Dickens racing, like Thackeray, against the printer.

Young people of both sexes who think they would like to "take up" writing (although nobody ever talks about "taking up" plumbing), and all those delightful persons who tell us so frequently that they feel quite sure they could write a book if only they had the time, should take warning from the history of these great novelists, and remember Trollope's remark concerning the result of his first four novels:

"As regarded remuneration for the time, stone-breaking would have done better."

The writer is, as Trollope pointed out in another place, a literary labourer, and those who dislike hard labour had better give up all thoughts of writing.

F.E.B.

CONTENTS

ILLUSTRATIONS

WILLIAM MAKEPEACE THACKERAY

(1811–1861)

WILLIAM MAKEPEACE THACKERAY

From the canvas by Samuel Laurence now in the
National Portrait Gallery

WILLIAM MAKEPEACE THACKERAY
(1811–1861)

THACKERAY was what, Charles Dickens and George Meredith would have loved to be: the son of an old and distinguished family, comfortably off in his young manhood, with charming relations and connections.

Several generations of Thackeray's immediate ancestors entered the service of the East India Company. By the time he was born this service had become a family tradition.

The Thackeray family could trace its ancestry back to a certain John de Thackra, who in 1336 held of the Abbot of St. Mary of Fountains a dwelling house and thirty acres of land at Hartwich. The Thackras remained the Thackras until Walter Thackeray, in the seventeenth century, adopted the modern spelling of the name, and settled at Hampsthwaite, near Knaresborough, in the West Riding of Yorkshire.

The Thackerays were now getting on in the world. In 1746 we find Thomas Thackeray, an old Etonian, becoming headmaster of Harrow. It was high time that Eton intervened to preserve Harrow from internal disruption. At that time the school had been practically ruined by a headmaster who drank heavily and led a disorderly life in general. He had brought Harrow so low that only thirty boys remained on the books.

Thomas Thackeray, bringing Etonian order and method into this alien chaos, saved Harrow from itself and preserved it for posterity. But for him there would have been no Eton-Harrow match at Lord's, and no old Harrovian top-hats for old Etonians to bash on this chosen battle-ground. Thomas Thackeray built up the school until it had a hundred and thirty scholars, and won golden opinions even from those who writhed under his rod. For instance, a certain Dr. Parr, one of his pupils, has left this opinion of him:

"Though a strict disciplinarian, he possessed much kindness of temper, and much suavity of manner. I have reason to love and revere him as a father as well as a master"; a memorable tribute from Harrow to Eton.

The Indian history of the Thackeray family really begins with Thomas Thackeray. His youngest child, William Makepeace, grandfather of the novelist (Makepeace was a family name among the Thackerays), entered the East India Company's service, the first of his clan to do so. He began in a lowly position in the Secretary's office at a salary of £80 a year, but by diligence and ability he rose to great heights. Finally, Warren Hastings made him Collector of the Frontier Province of Sylhet. There he so distinguished himself that in 1774 Hastings brought him back to Dacca as Third in Council.

William Makepeace the First founded the Anglo-Indian Thackeray family, who became Very Important Persons in their day. Not only did they play their part in India, but they exerted much influence in the Court of Directors of the East India Company at home. When it is remembered that at this period the East India Company monopolised the trade with India, it will be seen that the Thackerays were people of substance.

Thackeray's father was Richmond Thackeray, the second son of William Makepeace the first, who had twelve children, nine of whom went out to India. Thus eight of Thackeray's uncles and aunts, besides his father, were Anglo-Indians.

Richmond was born at South Mimms on September 1st, 1781. He went to Eton at the age of ten, and stayed there until the year 1796, when he was nominated to a writership in the Bengal Civil Service, and left Eton to be trained in accountancy. He arrived at Calcutta in 1798 and proceeded to live up to the family standards, for very soon he was made Collector of Midnapur, being promoted for efficiency in Persian and Arabic.

Richmond married Anne Becher in Calcutta on October 13th, 1810. Anne was one of the reigning Calcutta beauties, which defines the standing of the Thackerays in India, for a reigning Calcutta beauty could marry whom she pleased, and in addition to being beautiful Anne came of an old Bengal family. In the following December Richmond and Anne moved to the official residence at Alipur, for Richmond had been appointed Collector of the Twenty-Four Parganas, one of the highest posts in the Bengal Service. At Alipur their only child, William Makepeace Thackeray the novelist, was born on July 18th, 1811.

The marriage of Richmond and Anne ebbed swiftly to its close, for Richmond died only four years after his son's birth. Thackeray remained in India with his beautiful and greatly loved mother until early in 1817, when the time came for him to go to England. The parting from his mother, who remained in India, grieved the six-year-old child very deeply. He was never to see India again, and although he remembered the country in after life, the Anglo-Indian types in his novels, including Colonel Newcome, were drawn from members of the Oriental Club in Hanover Square.

Thackeray was fortunate in his parents. Probably he inherited his luxurious tastes and appreciation of art and letters from his father, though Richmond died too early to exert much influence over his little son. The Collector of the Twenty-Four Parganas would not find much leisure, between his official and social life, to spend in the nursery. From his mother Thackeray certainly learned to appreciate beautiful, witty, cultivated women, and to understand the part played in life by love.

The lovely Anne did not remain a widow long. She married as her second husband Major Henry Carmichael-Smyth, of the Royal Bengal Engineers. Thackeray wrote her affectionate letters, begging her to come to England with her new husband. When she returned in 1821 he remembered her perfectly.

Until he went to school he was happy in England. He lived with his great uncle, Peter Moore, Lord of the Manor of Hadley, and M.P. for Coventry. Great uncle and great nephew became great friends, and no wonder, for Thackeray must have been a charming, intelligent little boy, with all the easy friendliness of a child who has never wanted for anything. If he stood in danger of being spoiled by the luxury of living with a Lord of the Manor, the tendency was corrected when he went to stay with his mother's grandmother and aunt. These ladies lived much more simply in a house in the high street of Fareham, Hampshire.

Like Trollope, Thackeray found his schools purgatories on earth. His first was a small establishment at Southampton, typical of the rest, as he discovered later. It was, he said, "governed by a horrible little tyrant". Kneeling by the bed at night the small Thackeray would implore:

"Pray, God, I may dream of my mother." Summing up his stay there in after life, he concluded:

"What a dreadful place that private school was; cold, chilblains, bad dinners, not enough victuals, and caning awful!"

Perhaps traces of this establishment's regime showed on him in the holidays, for they took him away and sent him to another school, kept by a Dr. Turner at Chiswick. The change brought no improvement in his life. He felt so unhappy that he tried to run away, but turned back. In his twelfth year (1822), probably without enthusiasm owing to his past experiences, he arrived at Charterhouse School.

If he retained any illusions, the headmaster of Charterhouse, Dr. John Russell, whom Thackeray nicknamed "Rude Boreas", destroyed them at once. His welcome was not hospitable. He said to the school janitor:

"Take that boy and his box to the matron, and make my compliments to the junior master and tell him the boy knows nothing, and will just do for the lowest form."

Thus Dr. Russell lost the confidence of his new pupil for ever. Thackeray was a shy boy, and found Russell's bellowing and sarcasm unbearable until he became used to them. He wrote in after years, with Russell and himself in mind:

"Do not laugh at him writhing, and cause all the other boys to laugh. Remember your own young days at school, my friend—the tingling cheeks, burning ears, and bursting heart, and passion of desperate tears, with which you looked up, after having performed some blunder, whilst the Doctor held you up to public scorn before the class, and cracked his great clumsy jokes upon you, helpless and a prisoner. Better the block itself, and the Lictors with their Fasces of birchen twigs, than the maddening torture of those jokes."

At the beginning of his career at Charterhouse, Thackeray was in the Rev. Edward Penny's house, situated in Wilderness Row, Clerkenwell Road (Charterhouse had not then moved

out of London), and hated it. Here is his picture of life in the
Rev. Edward Penny's house:

"We were fifty boys in our boarding house, and had to wash
in a leaden trough, under a cistern, with lumps of fat, yellow
soap floating about in the ice and water."

This was hardly the life for a boy born in India, but he seems
to have survived it without any permanent ill effect.

However, the rigours of the Rev. Edward Penny's house
did not last for ever, because Thackeray became, later on, a
day boy. Yet he still hated Charterhouse, even when he was
seventeen and second monitor in Day Boys. It is hardly
credible that in after life he delighted to be present at Charterhouse on Founder's Day, and made his last attendance at this
celebration on December 12th, 1863, eleven days before his
death.

In Thackeray's youth the education at public schools was
almost entirely classical, and he found himself unpopular with
masters because he had no aptitude for the classics. He seems
to have adopted the principle "By their fruits ye shall know
them", for he wrote afterwards:

"When I saw a brute of a schoolmaster, whose mind was as
coarse-grained as any ploughboy's in Christendom; whose
manners were those of the most insufferable of heaven's
creatures, the English snob trying to turn gentleman . . . and
heard him roar out praises, and pump himself into enthusiasm
for, certain Greek poetry,—I say I had my doubts about the
genuineness of the article."

There spoke the descendant of that other William Makepeace,
whom Warren Hastings made Third in Council, and the son of
Richmond Thackeray, Collector of the Twenty-Four Parganas.

His school fellows also thought poorly of him. They did not
consider that he would "ever rise to the top of any tree by
climbing". Probably the congenital languor of an Anglo-
Indian child helped to give them that impression. He says
frankly of himself:

"I was not a brilliant boy at school—the only prize I ever
remember to have got was in a kind of lottery in which I was
obliged to subscribe with seventeen other competitors—and
of which the prize was a flogging. That I won. But I don't
think I carried off any other."

As a boy he was a great reader, and in class delighted to prop a favourite book behind a pile of classical volumes. His style was never influenced by the classics, and shows no traces of them. His models were Fielding, Steele, Addison (old Carthusians), Goldsmith and Sterne. To these he did honour in his lectures on *The English Humourists*.

He carried a life-long souvenir of Charterhouse in the form of a broken nose. His friend, G. S. Venables, broke it in a fight; it was set, and later the same boy broke it again.

Charterhouse, as we should expect, appears in his novels. Young Rawdon Crawley, Arthur Pendennis, Colonel Newcome, and other characters went there. Colonel Newcome ended his days as a Charterhouse pensioner:

"At the usual evening hour the Chapel bell began to toll, and Thomas Newcome's hands outside the bed feebly beat time. And just as the last bell struck, a peculiar sweet smile shone over his face, and he lifted up his head a little, and quickly said:

" 'Adsum!' and fell back. It was the word we used at school, when names were called; and lo! he, whose heart was as that of a little child, had answered to his name, and stood in the presence of the Master."

Major Carmichael-Smyth, Thackeray's stepfather, settled, on his return from India in 1825, as a gentleman farmer at Larkbeare, near Ottery St. Mary. Thackeray used to spend his holidays from Charterhouse there, and Larkbeare is described in *Pendennis*, the most autobiographical of his novels. He left Charterhouse on April 16th, 1828, and returned to Larkbeare. He was now a well-grown young man of seventeen, with an income of his own and the world before him. It must have seemed like heaven to be quit of the rigours of Charterhouse, and live happily at home with his mother, whom he adored, and his stepfather, with whom he seems to have lived on the most affectionate terms. As far as we can judge, the next few years were to be the happiest in his life.

He had the natural indolence of all charming people, heightened by his Indian birth and the traditions of a long line of Indian Civil Servants who, though they worked hard in their own lofty fashion, led the life of absolute monarchs as far as the amenities were concerned. So Thackeray, with

the sufferings and miseries of school life behind him, passed
a number of lazy months at home, before going up to Cambridge in 1829. The social life at Larkbeare represented
all that he could have asked, for Major and Mrs. Carmichael-
Smyth moved in the most desirable Devonshire society.

It must have seemed a great day in Thackeray's life when
Major Carmichael-Smyth took him to Cambridge. There
is no doubt that he loved his fellow creatures, as long as they
were his own kind of creature. It is difficult to picture him
slumming. And, unlike Disraeli, who confessed that he disliked clubs, not being fond of male society, and looked on a
men's dinner as the most indescribable form of boredom,
Thackeray liked being about with men. Save for his brief,
unfortunate marriage and, doubtless, the usual pre-marriage
escapades of a young man, women do not seem to have entered
a great deal into his life. He was devoted to his daughters,
whom he called "my little women", and he certainly formed a
great attachment, later in life, for Mrs. Brookfield, the wife
of his friend.

For companionship in after life he came to depend a great
deal on clubs.

He had been entered at Trinity College, and his rooms were
on the ground floor in the Great Court opposite the Master's
Lodge, on the left of the Great Gate.

Given his temperament, it was inevitable that at Cambridge
he made many friends, including Richard Monckton Milnes,
his life-long friend William Henry Brookfield, Fitzgerald and
Tennyson. In spite of the opinion of Greek poetry he had
expressed while at Charterhouse, he began to read Greek
with great industry, but soon tired of it. The truth is that until
he lost his money and became compelled to work in order to
live, he surrendered to his charming natural indolence. That
he disciplined himself in time to the regular drudgery of
writing is not astonishing. There are few harder workers than
the lazy man who has conquered his laziness.

At Cambridge he wrote charming, faintly ingenuous letters
to his mother, sometimes illustrating them with sketches,
since he was born with a natural gift for drawing. In these
he told her of all that he did that was fit for her to know. We
hear nothing of him as an athlete; there is no record even of

the tremendous walks so enjoyed by Dickens and Meredith. True, he was a horseman, but necessarily everyone of his period was a horseman to some extent. The horse provided the only means of transport. Thackeray belonged to the period when Lord Palmerston rode down to the House of Commons on his well-known grey, and trotted from his London house to Harrow for Speech Day within the hour.

At Cambridge, like so many undergraduates who afterwards became writers, Thackeray dabbled in University journalism. There were two publications to which he contributed, *The Snob* and *The Gownsman*. The first pretended to be written by non-University contributors; *The Gownsman* acknowledged that its talent was drawn from Cambridge men.

They were delightful days, but they did not last very long, because in June 1830 Thackeray came down from Cambridge without taking a degree. He brought with him his debts and his memories, but, besides cultivating the art of friendship, he had not altogether wasted his time. After giving up the study of Greek he read widely in English, chiefly poetry and old English novels. He was to become a purely native writer, for he owed nothing to the Greeks and the Romans, and everything to his forerunners in English literature.

A month after coming down from Cambridge he left England for a wander year on the Continent. It was not such an impressive itinerary as the Grand Tour of the contemporary young nobleman, but probably a great deal more amusing, for among other gifts Thackeray had the capacity for being amused highly developed.

He stayed first in Paris, and continued to Coblenz, and then to Godesberg, where he remained a month. From Godesberg he made a romantic journey by Rhine steamer to Cologne. Eventually he arrived at Weimar, which seemed to appeal to him, as he settled there for some time.

Weimar, of course, was sacred to Goethe, and there he met the great man.

"George Eliot" described the Weimar of her and Thackeray's days as "more like a huge village or market town than the precincts of a court". Perhaps its amorphous charms appealed to Thackeray; whatever the charm it held him. He attended the local Court, and indulged in social gaieties, and perhaps the spell Weimar cast upon him suggested, many years later, the idea for his lectures entitled *The Four Georges*.

He came home in the autumn of 1831, and to please his family, who wanted him to study law, entered the Middle Temple and began to read for the Bar. However, the law appealed to him as little as it did to Disraeli. Thackeray while reading lived at No. 2 Brick Court, at one time the chambers of Oliver Goldsmith, until he shared chambers at No. 10 Crown Office Row with Tom Taylor. It is recorded that while in the Temple he lost £1,500 through gambling.

He certainly had fun while a law student, his one sorrow being that his uncle, the Rev. Francis Thackeray, insisted on asking him to dinner three times a week. Thackeray would have preferred to avoid crabbed age and consort with youth. There is a picture of his life at this period in *Pendennis*, but for all his amusements his hatred of law increased to the point when he gave it up and retreated to Paris. In December 1832 he returned to Larkbeare. He was now twenty-one, and had inherited capital which produced an income of £500 a year. It was enough for bread and butter, but he realised that he would need to work if he wanted jam on his bread and butter.

Having decided finally that his profession should be literature, he bought, in 1833, a newly established paper called the *National Standard*, of which he became editor and proprietor. The paper died in a few months, causing him a loss of £200. Two years after he inherited it his fortune had disappeared, partly through his love of gambling, partly from settling Cambridge debts, and partly through the failure of an Indian Bank. Years afterwards he pointed out a certain gambler in a street in Spa.

"I have not seen him," he said, "since he drove me down in his cabriolet to my bankers in the City, where I sold out my patrimony and handed it over to him."

After the disastrous failure of the *National Standard*, he carried on a brief flirtation with art. It has been said that he was born with a natural gift for drawing. He returned to Paris in order to study art, living in the Rue des Beaux Arts, and leading the same gay, care-free life that he had lived in the Temple. After a time he discovered that he would never become a painter. Consequently he left Paris for England to make a fresh start. In the year 1836 he asked to be allowed to illustrate the *Pickwick Papers*, then appearing in monthly numbers, but nothing came of it. Had he succeeded, the fact of one great novelist's illustrating the first successful work of another would have made artistic and literary history. However, he did not bury his artistic talent; in due time he illustrated his own works and contributed hundreds of sketches to *Punch*.

In the same year (1836) two important events in his life occurred. In spring, the season of hope, Major Carmichael-Smyth, with the easy optimism in matters of which he is quite ignorant typical of the retired Regular Army officer, founded a radical newspaper called *Constitutional*. His ideas were large. The paper was to advocate the ballot, triennial parliaments, freedom of the Press, religious freedom, and equality. Major Carmichael-Smyth appointed Thackeray his Paris correspondent, at a salary of £400 a year, so Thackeray found himself in Paris once more. He also fell in love with Isabella Getkin Creagh Shawe, and got married on the strength of his salary as Paris correspondent of *Constitutional*.

Bishop Luscombe married them at the British Embassy in Paris on April 20th, 1836. Thackeray's friend, Henry Reeve, described Isabella as " a nice, simple, girlish girl; a niece of old Colonel Shawe". Thackeray, who always advocated young, improvident marriages, certainly lived up to his theory. The young couple lived happily in the Rue Neuve St. Augustin, while *Constitutional* staggered onward to its inevitable doom.

Thackeray's first Paris despatch appeared in the issue for September 19th, 1836, and his last in that for February 15th, 1837. *Constitutional* died on July 1st, 1837, its death almost coinciding with the accession of Queen Victoria on June 20th of that year. Poor Major Carmichael-Smyth, like so many retired Regular officers who dabble in the Unknown, lost most of his money.

There being no point in his remaining in Paris after the death of his paper, Thackeray brought his wife back to London, where they lived at No. 13 Great Coram Street. In this house were born their eldest daughter Anne Isabella, afterwards Lady Ritchie, and a second daughter, Jane, who died in infancy, as did a multitude of Victorian children.

For a time, the marriage was happy. Thackeray, no longer a salaried member of the staff of *Constitutional*, looked about for literary work, not without success. Mrs. Thackeray had one extremely useful relation from her husband's point of view, none other than Thomas Barnes, the famous editor of *The Times*, and in its issue of August 3rd, 1837, appeared Thackeray's review of Carlyle's *French Revolution*. In this year also he began his connection with *Fraser's Magazine* which, together with his work for *Punch*, laid the foundation of his success as a writer.

By 1837 he was a member of the staff of *Fraser's*, and a regular contributor. For it he wrote the *Letters of Mr. C. J. Yellowplush*, *Catherine*, and *The Great Hoggarty Diamond*. His *Snob Papers* in *Punch* coincided with that paper's upward curve of circulation owing to the popularity of Leech's drawings.

Thackeray, when only a beginner, had learned that the two canons of success for a writer are to spread his net wide as regards subjects and not to put all his eggs in one basket as regards publishers. Thus, when the editor of the *Edinburgh Review* suggested that he should write for it, he replied:

"I hardly know what subject to point out as suited to my capacity—light matter connected with art, humorous subjects, critique of novels—French subjects, memoirs, poetry, history from Louis XV downward and of an earlier period—that of Froissart and Monstrelet—German literature and poetry—though of these I know little beyond what I learned in a year's residence in the country fourteen years ago."

He added that he "preferred writing on subjects relating to society in general, where a writer may be allowed to display the humorous *ego*, or a victim to be gently immolated".

This at any rate gave an editor a certain choice, and an idea of the young writer's scope. In not a very long while Thackeray found himself doing a great deal of work for magazines and reviews, but the high note in this type of work was struck by the *Yellowplush Letters*.

The year 1840 dealt him a blow from which he could never recover, which affected the whole of his life. In that year his third daughter, Harriet Marion, later Mrs. Leslie Stephen, was born on May 28th. After his daughter's birth he left for Belgium to collect material for a Belgian Sketch Book. While there he received a summons to return home on account of his wife's health.

He found her in "a strange state of languor and mental inactivity". Horrified by these symptoms, he sent his children to his mother, and took his wife to her parents in Ireland. Later she spent some time in an asylum in Paris, and when she came out he travelled with her in the vain hope that change of scene would restore her mind. When it became clear that she would never be cured, he placed her with a Mr. and Mrs. Thompson at Leigh, in Essex. She outlived her husband by many years, and died at Leigh in 1894, aged seventy-six.

Thus, while still a young man, Thackeray became homeless and wifeless with two little daughters in his charge. He could not marry again while his wife remained alive, and she was to live longer than he. As a result, much of his life came to be passed in clubs and hotels.

In 1840 Macrone published a collection of Thackeray's work entitled, "*The Paris Sketch Book.* By Mr. Titmarsh." It did not make any great sensation. Macrone's successor published "*Comic Tales and Sketches.* Edited and illustrated by Mr. Michael Angelo Titmarsh" in 1841. After that Thackeray transferred to Chapman & Hall, a firm of which we shall hear so much in this book, who published *The Irish Sketch Book* in 1843, his first successful book. This also he signed "Michael Angelo Titmarsh", but in the dedication to Charles Lever he signed himself W. M. Thackeray for the first time in any book. In 1842 he had made a tour in Ireland, when he met Lever and formed a friendship with him. The *Irish Sketch Book* is one of Thackeray's most charming travel books.

Chapman & Hall commissioned a second book of sketches, entitled *From Cornhill to Cairo*, and this book took him far away. The P. & O. Steamship Company presented him with a free passage, doubtless having excellent publicity for the Line in view, and Thackeray sailed East on the first of his several voyages. What with his free passage and the work he did while away the voyage must have paid him very well. Apart from making notes for the Chapman & Hall book, he contributed articles to *Punch*, under the title of "*Punch* in the East", and finished what was called originally *The Luck of Barry Lyndon*, which had started appearing serially at the beginning of the year (1844) in *Fraser's Magazine,* and was titled in book form, *Memoirs of Barry Lyndon.*

The change of title arose from Thackeray's habit of many pen-names. In *Fraser's Magazine* the authorship of *Barry Lyndon* was attributed to Mr. Fitzboodle, but the book appeared as "*Memoirs of Barry Lyndon:* Written by Himself".

For what my opinion is worth, *Barry Lyndon* is my favourite Thackeray novel, though *Pendennis* runs it close. The hero seems to me one of the most fascinating scoundrels in fiction, and the book is written with an unsurpassed vitality and spirit. It is not a pleasant story, and Thackeray said of it to his elder daughter: "You need not read it. You would not like it."

Barry Lyndon was finished at Malta on November 3rd, 1844. Thackeray reached England in December, and in 1845 wrote his travel book, now called *From Cornhill to Grand Cairo,* and illustrated it with his own sketches. He signed it "M. A. Titmarsh" and it appeared in January 1846.

It was now about eight years since he had begun writing, and although reasonably prosperous he had by no means attained fame. His shorter work, his articles and art and literary criticism, pleased editors, but they did not care for his fiction, and neither did the public. The *Yellowplush Letters* still marked the peak of the curve; since then it had dropped. Readers did not care particularly either for *The Great Hoggarty Diamond, Catherine,* or *Barry Lyndon.* Thackeray was earning money and his expenses as a bachelor did not necessarily amount to a great deal, but he had the expenses of his insane wife and his daughters' education to meet.

He still maintained complete faith in himself, but by comparison with his contemporaries he lagged behind. He was now thirty-five; Harrison Ainsworth published *Rookwood* at twenty-nine, and Disraeli *Vivian Grey* at twenty-two; by the time he reached thirty-three *Vivian Grey* had been followed by *The Young Duke, Contarini Fleming, Alroy, Henrietta Temple* and *Venetia.* Dickens at twenty-four wrote *Sketches by Boz,* and *Pickwick* at twenty-five.

At thirty-five Thackeray's reputation rested on work in magazines for the most part. He suffered badly from the use of too many pen-names: Michael Angelo Titmarsh wrote reviews, short stories and *The Great Hoggarty Diamond*; Yellow-plush wrote the correspondence; Ikey Solomons wrote *Catherine*; and Mr. Fitzboodle *Barry Lyndon* and other work. A great many of his contributions were anonymous, and he signed contributions to *Punch* with various names.

All this does not make for fame, or cause an author to stick in a reader's memory, but Thackeray and probably his editors realised that he wrote far too much for the mass of it to be attributed to one name only, for fear of surfeiting the reader.

Another handicap to fame resided in the fact that he insisted on keeping his own standards. Dickens delighted to play to the gallery, but Thackeray refused.

His domestic life, during this period of heavy work, seems, as we look back on it, pathetically haphazard and unappealing. He was in the state into which the kind of man who needs a woman to look after him gets when there is no woman to look after him.

When his wife's mind failed he gave up his house, and took a room at No. 27 Jermyn Street, that street sacred to bachelors. Henry Vizetelly, who called on him here in 1843, found him in the front room at the top of the house, and has left this picture of what he saw:

"A tall, slim individual between thirty and thirty-five years of age, with a pleasant, smiling countenance, and a bridgeless nose, and clad in a dressing-gown of decided Parisian cut, rose from a small table standing close to the near window to receive me. When he stood up the low pitch of the room caused him to look even taller than he really was, and his actual height was well over six feet. . . .

"The apartment was an exceedingly plainly furnished bed-room, with common rush-seated chairs and painted French bedstead, and with neither looking-glass nor prints on the bare, cold, cheerless-looking walls. On the table from which Mr. Thackeray had risen a white cloth was spread, on which was a frugal breakfast tray, a cup of chocolate and some dry toast; and huddled together at the other end were some writing materials, two or three numbers of *Fraser's Magazine*, and a few slips of manuscript."

Vizetelly, who was founding the *Pictorial Times*, had called to ask Thackeray to contribute to his new paper. He goes on:

"Mr. Thackeray at once undertook to write upon art, to review such books as he might fancy, and to contribute an occasional article on the Opera . . . so satisfied was he with the three guineas offered him for a couple of columns weekly that he jocularly expressed himself willing to sign an agreement for life on these terms. I can only suppose . . . that the prospect of an additional hundred and sixty pounds to his income was, at that moment, anything but a matter of indifference. The humble quarters in which he was installed seemed at any rate to indicate that, for some reason or other, strict economy was just then the order of the day with him."

What Thackeray needed was a literary agent who, in his sober but rich office, would have received Vizetelly and explained how desperately busy Mr. Thackeray was with a multitude of commissioned work, and how he could not possibly accept less than three guineas a column from Mr. Vizetelly. The literary agent would have charged commission, but even then Thackeray's profits would have increased greatly. No ambitious writer should ever receive an editor or publisher in humble quarters which seem to indicate that strict economy is the order of the day with him. If he is poor and must meet the editor he should meet him in his agent's sober but rich office.

Or, of course, Thackeray might have given Vizetelly luncheon at one of his clubs, which would have impressed him and been well worth the cost of his food and drink. At the age of twenty-one, Thackeray had been elected to the Garrick Club, and in 1840 to the Reform Club. In 1851 he was elected to the Athenæum. Even if an author lives in a Jermyn Street bed-sitting-room, he can create quite a startling effect at one of these eminent institutions, and no editor or publisher need, or should, ever know about the bed-sitting-room.

Being a bachelor, with only a bed-sitting-room to go home to, Thackeray depended greatly on clubs. He did not confine his society to the venerable mausoleums mentioned above. He was fond of Bohemian society, though not if it was rough and frowsy. His long line of ancestors in the Indian Civil Service had transmitted to him their taste for orderly proceedings and a touch of ceremonial. But there was a little club on the first floor of a public house in Dean Street, Soho, which he liked, and he was also seen a good deal at Evans's, run by John Green in Covent Garden, a great meeting place in those days for men about Town. It was Evans's which suggested the "Cave of Harmony" in *The Newcomes*.

Just as the *Yellowplush Letters* marked the first turning point in Thackeray's career, so *Vanity Fair* marked the turning point in his fiction. Like a great many lesser authors, he sometimes had ideas in the night, and the title "Vanity Fair" occurred to him in the middle of the night when he was writing the book at the Old Ship Hotel, Brighton. On account of his homelessness he did much work in clubs and hotels.

He sold *Vanity Fair* to Bradbury & Evans, of whom also we shall hear much more, in 1846. Like Dickens's novels, it was to appear in monthly numbers, at a price of fifty guineas a number, this price to include the letterpress, two etchings, and chapter initials.

There is an unshakable belief among the non-writing public that all respectable authors, especially great authors, write with immense slowness and seriousness, weighing every word, polishing and repolishing, tearing up what they have written and writing it over again. This is not so, as will be made plain to anyone who reads this book. The picking and choosing, the selection and rejection, are done while the author is constructing his novel. When he begins to write, with the construction done, he may write as quickly as he likes, or as quickly as he can, for some authors write more slowly than others. Disraeli, for one, laid it down that once the construction is completed the more rapid the execution the better.

According to Vizetelly, *Vanity Fair*, which made Thackeray's name as a novelist, was written to a large extent "under great pressure from the printer", some of it while the printer's boy waited in the hall for copy. What astonishes a modern author is not the capacity of the Victorian novelist, but the happy-go-lucky optimism of the Victorian publishers, who began light-heartedly to issue a novel in monthly numbers long before it was finished. It never seems to have occurred to them that a passing cab might have projected the author into the next world as he crossed the street, and left them with an unfinished novel some of which had been sold serially.

The first number of *Vanity Fair* appeared in January 1847,

and nobody seemed very interested. In fact, the lack of interest so impressed the publishers that they debated whether publication should be stopped. As the year went on, the novel became a glittering success, some say because the *Edinburgh Review* praised it, others because Charlotte Brontë dedicated the second edition of *Jane Eyre* to Thackeray. The genius of the author may also have had something to do with his success.

Miss Brontë wrote in her dedication:

"Why have I alluded to this man? I have alluded to him, Reader, because I think I see in him an intelligence profounder and more unique (*sic*) than his contemporaries have yet recognised. . . ."

Mrs. Carlyle wrote joyfully to her husband that *Vanity Fair* "Beat Dickens out of the world". Yet at its highest circulation about 7,000 copies a month were sold, whereas Dickens sold 25,000 copies a month at times.

A critic has written of *Vanity Fair*:

"*Vanity Fair* . . . was not only something amazingly new to the public; its author was practically an unknown man. In this great novel Thackeray found his range and addressed the world. There was a peculiar significance in describing the book as 'a Novel without a Hero'; it was in the nature of a challenge. The novelists of the day, while professing to deal with life as it is, put forth the conventionalised hero and painted in the theatrical back-cloth to suit him, evading the facts of life with a bland indifference to truth or verisimilitude. Thackeray would sweep away the cult of sham heroics and sham sentiment then fashionable in fiction.

"Such was his professed aim in writing *Vanity Fair*. It implied a new kind of novel—new, that is to say, to a generation that had forgotten Fielding and neglected Miss Austen. And like the great master with whose genius he had so much affinity, with much of Fielding's serene detachment from any kind of *parti pris*, with a knowledge and command of his material comparable only with Fielding, he takes the world as the stage of his social comedy."

It is perhaps a compliment to Thackeray's powers of observation that women complained about his women characters, for women always complain if too closely and accurately observed, and described with candour. Charlotte Brontë thought him "unjust to women—quite unjust", despite the dedication of *Jane Eyre*. Harriet Martineau wrote:

"The first drawback in his books, as in his manners, is the impression conveyed by both that he can never have known a good and sensible woman." He must indeed have pierced Harriet between the joints of her armour to arouse such bitterness.

As is usual in the case of an author of an outstanding book, Thackeray became a social lion, and a personage. This both amused and pleased him; he came of too good a family to be attracted by the attentions of hostesses, but he liked people and company, and dinners and social occasions. He told Lady Blessington, after the success of *Vanity Fair*, that he had "reeled from dinner party to dinner party, wallowed in turtle, and swum in claret and champagne." Why he reeled and wallowed, if he did reel and wallow, but this sounds very unlike the fastidious Thackeray, he explained to another woman friend. He said:

"If I don't go out and mingle in society I can't write." He wanted the stir and comfort of a crowd, for he was a lonely man except for the society of his two young daughters. He liked the rich appurtenances of the rich, and in consequence was accused of being a tuft-hunter, but the description hardly fits him. He was ill and overworked, often suffering pain from an internal complaint, and he longed for gaiety and distraction.

However, the circumstances of his home life improved after his return from Cairo. He then gave up the unattractive Jermyn Street bed-sitting-room in which Vizetelly had found him, and took chambers in St. James's Street. The outlook of St. James's Street even now is very different from that of Jermyn Street, and in Thackeray's day the difference was still more marked. In the summer of 1846 he took a house for himself and his daughters at No. 13 (now No. 16) Young Street, Kensington, and wrote much of *Vanity Fair* there. He was now in a position to offer hospitality at home. In due time Charlotte Brontë dined there, but the party was a failure.

George Smith, the publisher, introduced them in 1849. Charlotte expected a prophet, and found an English gentleman, a very different thing. She sat opposite him at the dinner party, and according to Thackeray's version of the proceedings, which may or may not be a little embroidered for the sake of telling a good story, saw her ideal of him shattered as everything went into his mouth and nothing came out of it in the way of conversation.

"At last," he said, "as I took my fifth potato, she leaned across with clasped hands and tearful eyes, and breathed imploringly:

" 'Oh, Mr. Thackeray! Don't!' "

This story is probably true in spirit if not in detail, for Charlotte could never understand him. She told a woman friend:

"He was a Titan of mind. I felt sufficiently at ease with all but Thackeray; with him I was fearfully stupid."

Perhaps the combination of a six-foot-three presence and a brilliant wit crushed poor Charlotte. Perhaps Thackeray felt bored and showed it. He was capable of leaving a party given by himself in his own house, and disappearing to another room never to return, if his guests bored him.

Only the most self-satisfied author escapes the fear that his popularity may vanish and his public with it, and Thackeray did not suffer from the weakness of self-satisfaction. He had now reached the age of thirty-nine, he had worked desperately hard, and in spite of his impressive appearance did not enjoy robust health. He possessed liabilities in his daughters and his mentally deficient wife and was not getting any younger. It occurred to him that he might do worse than effect some sort of insurance against his possible disappearance as a writer. Accordingly he had himself called to the Bar, so that he could be a candidate for a Government appointment reserved for barristers. In trying to obtain such an appointment he met with no success, which was fortunate for posterity, but a source of anxiety to him.

Realising that it must be authorship or nothing, he took his daughters abroad for a holiday and then returned to Brighton and began to write *Pendennis* which, as has been explained, is the most autobiographical of his novels. This, like *Vanity Fair*, was published by Bradbury & Evans in monthly parts, beginning in November 1848. Publication continued until September 1849, when Thackeray became seriously ill.

His illness continued until the following November, and it

seemed likely that he would die, but in December there came an improvement. His determination is illustrated by the fact that the twelfth number of *Pendennis* appeared in January 1849.

Pendennis completed its serialisation in December 1850 and it was then that Thackeray discovered the second string to his bow which a Government appointment had failed to provide, and decided to lecture. He approached the prospect with distaste and a certain amount of nervousness, but he wanted money. His ambition was to provide for his daughters, mother, and stepfather, and for himself if he lived to be old, although the doctors had told him that he would never live to reach old age.

The subject of his lectures was *The English Humorists of the Eighteenth Century*, one of the most charming series of essays ever written, but he must have written them *con amore*, for the eighteenth century represented his spiritual home. There were six lectures, and he delivered the first at Willis's Rooms on May 21st, 1851, the charge for the series being £2 2s. or 7s. 6d. for an unreserved seat at one lecture.

Lady Ritchie, his daughter, wrote in her biographical introduction to the centenary edition of these lectures:

"As one reads the lectures on the Humorists, one feels how much my father was at ease with all these people, whom he loved and admired. He trod in the actual footsteps of Johnson and Goldsmith, and Steele and Addison. He saw the things they had seen, heard the echoes to which they had listened, he walked up the very streets where they had walked. He was one of them, and happy in their good company. Sir Walter Scott also wrote of these times, also admired and appreciated all these personalities, but he belonged to a different and more romantic world of chivalry and adventure. As for my father— so he says in one of his letters—'the eighteenth century occupies him to the exclusion almost of the nineteenth', and he carried its traditions along with him."

The day before the first lecture Thackeray wrote to his friend Richard Doyle:

"MY DEAR D:

I hope you will come to the tight-rope exhibition to-morrow, and send you a card. You and your friend will please sit in distant parts of the room.

When you see me put my hand to my watch-chain, you will say:

'God bless my soul, how beautiful!'

When I touch my neck-cloth clap with all your might.

When I use my pocket-handkerchief burst into tears.

When I pause, say Brah-ah-ah-ahvo, through the pause.

You had best bring with you a very noisy umbrella; to be used at proper intervals: and if you can't cry at the pathetic parts, please blow your nose very hard.

And now, everything having been done to insure success that mortal can do, the issue is left to the immortal Gods.

God save the Queen. No money returned. Babies in arms NOT admitted.

By yours ever,
W. M. T."

Mrs. Kemble has told the story of how nervous Thackeray became immediately before the lecture started, and how she tried to comfort him, and how just before he was to begin to read she dropped his manuscript from the desk, and the pages lay in disorder on the floor. All Thackeray said was that she had given him occupation and distraction in sorting the manuscript during the ten minutes he still had to wait.

As all who have read *The English Humorists* will find it easy to believe, the lectures were a triumphant success. Even Macaulay, who attended the whole series, approved of them. The audience at Willis's Rooms included Charlotte Brontë, Mr. and Mrs. Brookfield, Mr. and Mrs. Carlyle, Richard Doyle, Cruikshank, Millais, Landseer, Dickens, and other Victorian celebrities. Charlotte Brontë, as may be imagined, wrote a flowing report of the lectures to her father.

Thackeray, famous as a novelist, had found fame once more as a lecturer. He toured England and was invited to lecture in the United States. He became very tired of lecturing, but he found it a rest from writing, and earned far more money than he could have earned by writing in the same time. In January 1852 he notes:

"They make me an offer of £150 at the Portman Square Rooms—pretty well for six hours." Sometimes the audience disappointed him. He wrote from Liverpool:

"Not above two hundred people came to the lectures, and the Philharmonic Hall, the most beautiful room I've seen, is made for two thousand five hundred, so that the little audience shudders in the middle, and the lecturer stands in a vast empty orchestra where there is a place for one hundred and fifty musicians."

At the same time he was writing *Esmond*, which he wished to finish before leaving for the United States, where he had decided at last to lecture.

One critic at least considers *Esmond* "a novel beyond question first of its class in English fiction, and also, I am inclined to think, the finest of all the productions of its author".

Perhaps *Esmond* succeeded so brilliantly because the scene is the age of Queen Anne, in which no one could feel more at home than Thackeray. Steele, Addison, and Swift are introduced, all three of them almost personal friends of the author. Unlike *Pendennis* and *Vanity Fair*, it did not appear in monthly numbers; according to Thackeray it was "much too grave and sad for that". He also said that *Esmond* was the very best he could do. Authors are often wrong about the value of a particular work, but in this case Thackeray made no mistake.

He did not look forward in the least to his American adventure. English writers had become most unpopular in the United States since the descent there of Dickens (q.v.), for Dickens had lampooned the United States and Americans in *American Notes*, written after his return to England. The Americans in the end, with true national chivalry and kindness of heart, decided to be fair to Thackeray, forget about Dickens, and take Thackeray on his merits.

Finally, he wrote to a friend:

"There is a Boston boat sails on October 30th (1852), and that will carry Titmarsh and his lectures."

The voyage across the Atlantic shook Thackeray. Though Lowell and Arthur Hugh ("Say not the struggle naught availeth") Clough were on board, he loathed the discomfort of the voyage. He tried to write a little with a pencil when he had recovered from sea-sickness, but complained in a letter home that the ship pitched so he could not write, and even his sentences lurched about. Nobody, he declared, really likes the sea, and the captain and all liked the fireside at home a thousand times better.

He found it remarkable that the captain found Halifax in the end:

"So that we come three thousand miles over the enormous pathless ocean, through storm and darkness, with many a day no sun to make observations by, and the captain knows within fifteen minutes when we shall see a particular little rock with a light on it."

In the United States well-known men greeted him—Dana and Horace Greeley, Washington Irving, George Curtis, Bayard Taylor. In New York he settled in a good hotel ("up three pairs of stairs"; how different from the New York of today, when the express lifts make their first stop at the seventeenth floor) and two thousand people came every night to his lectures. The people, he wrote, did not turn out with flags and drums to receive him like Dickens, but the welcome was a most pleasant one.

Motley wrote of him:

"His enunciation is perfect. Every word he uttered might have been heard in the remotest quarters of the room, yet he scarcely lifted his voice above a colloquial tone." Thackeray became so much at ease in the United States that he said at a dinner that he only found Englishmen there, to which a distinguished American replied that in Mr. Thackeray they found a genuine Yankee. Could international accord have gone further?

The rewards of lecturing delighted him. From Boston he announced that he left behind nearly £1,000 in New York, "so that my girls will be very considerably better for the journey."

The Hon. William B. Reed, an American diplomat, asked him for his candid opinion of the United States, and he replied:

"Now, that which most impressed me here is, that I find homes as pure as ours, firesides like ours, domestic virtues as gentle; the English language, though the accent be a little different, with its homelike melody; and the Common Prayer Book in your families. I am more struck by pleasant resemblances than anything else."

From his first lecture tour in the United States he made at least £2,500, and the fees probably amounted to a great deal more. Like most lecturers, he became very tired of lecturing, the constant travelling, the publicity, and the horde of strangers who must be met everywhere, on whom he must make the right impression. He endured it only that he might leave his daughters secure financially.

Suddenly he could bear the strain no longer. On April 20th, 1853, he said to his secretary, who had made bookings for lectures in the west and middle west:

"There's a Cunarder going this morning. I'll see if I can get berths in her." He succeeded, sailed that day, and reached Liverpool six months after leaving. His eldest daughter has left a moving account of his homecoming:

"I can still remember sitting with my grandparents expecting his return. My sister and I sat on the red sofa in the little study, and shortly before the time we had calculated he might arrive came a little ring at the front door bell.

"My grandmother broke down; my sister and I rushed to the front door, only we were so afraid that it might not be he that we dared not open it, and there we stood until a second and much louder ring brought us to our senses.

" 'Why didn't you open the door?' said my father, stepping in, looking well, broad, and upright, laughing. In a moment he had never been away at all."

There was not to be much more of Young Street and the little study with the red sofa. That year (1853) Thackeray moved to 36 Onslow Square. He lived there for seven years, and there wrote *The Four Georges*, *The Virginians*, and the last part of *The Newcomes*, among other works. He finished *The Newcomes* in 1854, and the novel brought him additional fame. It is more tenderly written than its predecessors, and has a certain melancholy. The passage describing Colonel Newcome's end has been quoted, and on this high plane the rest of the story moves.

The Virginians was a sequel to *Esmond*, but Thackeray could do little wrong by this time, even in a sequel. The charm and the genius are still there.

Having established himself in the Onslow Square House, he went abroad for a time with his daughters. He fell ill again in London in 1854, and perhaps on that account, feeling, possibly, that his health might not be able to stand the strain of a writer's life, asked for the secretaryship of the British Legation in Washington. His request was not granted, and Lord Clarendon gave the post to someone else.

The first number of *The Newcomes* was published in October 1853, and the last in August 1855. He went abroad again in the summer of 1855, and it proved an unlucky journey, for in Rome he fell ill with a fever from which he never made a complete recovery. Back in London he began to write a new series of American Lectures, *The Four Georges*.

Historically these have their faults. Thackeray was unjust to poor Sophia Dorothea of Hanover who, if she took Count von Königsmarck for a lover could offer the excuse of being tied to a horrible husband, George Louis, son of the Elector of Hanover, afterwards George I. She was as much sinned against as sinning, and into the bargain her mother-in-law, Sophia of Hanover, never gave her a moment's peace. Thackeray also, whenever he had an opportunity, played down to the exterior morality, as opposed to the secret immorality, of the Victorians, and even dragged in Mary Queen of Scots, who has nothing whatever to do with the four Georges, in order to complain that she had been whitewashed by Agnes Strickland, the historian, just as others had whitewashed Sophia Dorothea.

Apart from these details, *The Four Georges* and *The English Humorists* seem to me to represent Thackeray's best work. Perhaps because of his early familiarity with Germany, and his long stay at Weimar, he reproduces the very atmosphere of little German courts, and we feel that we know them as well as he did. He explained his secret when he wrote in the lecture on George I:

"I like to people the old world with its everyday figures and inhabitants—not so much with heroes fighting immense battles and inspiring repulsed battalions to engage; or statesmen locked up in darkling cabinets and meditating ponderous laws and due conspiracies—as with people occupied with their everyday work or pleasure; my lord and lady hunting in the forest, or dancing in the court, or bowing to their Serene Highnesses as they pass in to dinner; John Cook and his procession bringing the meal from the kitchen; the jolly butlers bearing in the flagons from the cellar; the stout coachman driving the ponderous gilt wagon, with eight cream-coloured horses in housings of scarlet velvet and morocco leather; a postilion on the leaders, and a pair or a half-dozen of running footmen scudding along by the side of the vehicle, with conical caps, long silver-headed maces, which they poised as they ran, and splendid jackets laced all over with gold and silver.

"I fancy the citizens' wives and their daughters looking out from the balconies; and the burghers over their beer and mumm, rising up, cap in hand, as the cavalcade passes through the town with torch-bearers, trumpeters blowing their lusty cheeks out, and squadrons of jack-booted lifeguardsmen, girt with shining cuirasses, and bestriding thundering chargers, escorting his Highness's coach from Hanover to Herrenhausen; or halting, maybe, at Madame Platen's country house of Monplaisir, which lies half-way between the summer-palace and the Residenz."

This sort of thing gives even the uninstructed the chance of assimilating the picture of the Elector of Hanover and the life he lived. Thackeray was never, in his lectures, unmindful of his public. Unlike Dickens, he wished to please United States audiences, and as he did not like George IV, offered him up as a sacrifice to the Americans in the closing lines of his George IV lecture:

"Which was the most splendid spectacle ever witnessed— the opening feast of Prince George (George IV) in London, or the resignation of Washington? Which is the noble character for after ages to admire,—yon fribble dancing in lace and spangles, or yonder hero who sheathes his sword after a life of spotless honour, a purity unreproached, a courage indomitable, and a consummate victory? Which of these is the true gentleman?

"What is to be a gentleman? Is it to have lofty aims, to lead a pure life, to keep your honour virgin; to have the esteem of your fellow citizens, and the love of your fireside; to bear good fortune meekly; to suffer evil with constancy; and through evil or good to maintain truth always? Show me the happy man whose life exhibits these qualities, and him we will salute as gentleman, whatever his rank may be; show me the prince who possesses them, and he may be sure of our love and loyalty.

"The heart of Britain still beats kindly for George III, not because he was wise and just, but because he was pure in life, honest in intent, and because according to his lights he worshipped heaven. I think we acknowledge to the inheritrix of his sceptre (Queen Victoria) a wiser rule and a life as honourable and pure; and I am sure the future painter of our manners will pay a willing allegiance to that good life, and be loyal to the memory of that unsullied virtue."

No doubt his American audiences, who worshipped George Washington, and approved of Queen Victoria, clapped this peroration to the echo, and went home and told their friends what a fine fellow Thackeray was.

His friends gave him a farewell dinner on October 11th, 1855, at the London Tavern, on the occasion of his second voyage to the United States as a lecturer. Dickens took the Chair, and it was the kind of party Thackeray loved. He sailed on October 13th, the American welcome was lavish, they took *The Four Georges* to their hearts, and he made far more money than during his first lecture tour. He wrote home:

"I shall make all but £1,000 in five weeks, though not, of course, to continue at this rate."

His second departure from the United States was just as sudden as his first. In both cases he seems to have felt, on impulse, that he could not bear lecturing in the United States any longer.

"Friday 25th" (of April 1856), he noted, "as I walked down Broadway seeming very bright, warm, and cheery, I went with my usual sudden impetus straight into Collins's office, and was off the next day before I knew I was gone."

Perhaps he realised instinctively that he had not many more years to live and felt the call of home. However, his return did not stop the money-making properties of *The Four Georges*. He lectured in London and the provinces, and the lectures brought him fifty guineas apiece.

The year following his return to England saw the most peculiar adventure of his career. He was invited to stand for Oxford as a Liberal candidate. He commented in a letter:

"Today I get invitations (to lecture) from Ireland, declined with thanks; from Devonshire, from Bath again, and Bristol and from Yorkshire for the summer. Where is this going to stop? . . . just when the novel-writing faculty is pretty well used up, here is Independence, a place in Parliament, and who knows what afterwards? Upon my word, I don't seem much to care, and Fate carries me along in a stream somehow. Shall I float with it, or jump in shore? I shan't be happy in politics, and they'll interfere with my digestion; but with the game there it seems faint-hearted not to play it. 'Retire and paint pooty little pictures!' says Ease; perhaps Conscience, 'Retire and work at literature, at history!' "

Destiny took the decision out of his hands. He was defeated by 1085 to 1018.

In 1858 came the historic quarrel with Dickens.

It arose over an article on Thackeray published by Edmund Yates in his paper *Town Talk*. The article came near to being scurrilous, and nowadays would certainly have become the subject of a libel action. Thackeray wrote Yates a letter of complaint, and a letter by Yates in reply was redrafted by Dickens, to whom Yates showed it. Thackeray, being very annoyed, sent the correspondence to the Committee of the Garrick Club, to which Yates also belonged. The Committee, after considering the matter, gave Yates a time limit within which to apologise to Thackeray. Yates refused, and the Committee removed his name from the list of members.

Dickens then wrote to Thackeray offering to mediate, and Thackeray replied coldly that he had left the matter to the Committee of the Garrick Club. In consequence, the friendship between Dickens and Thackeray ceased to exist. However, shortly before Thackeray's death he met Dickens and offered him his hand, so that the quarrel ended.

During the year following this unfortunate affair (1859), Smith, Elder & Co. evolved the plan of founding a high-class shilling magazine, and offered Thackeray £350 a month for the serial rights of a novel. After this they offered him the editorship at £1,000 a year, and he accepted the offer. It was he who suggested the title *Cornhill Magazine*. The aim of the publishers was high; they decided that the magazine must be written by "scholars and gentlemen". They also wanted new authors, but, like all publishers starting a new magazine, had to fall back on the old brigade, because the public cannot be tempted with unknown names.

Consequently, contributors to the new *Cornhill Magazine* were drawn from the old contemporary gang: Thackeray, Trollope, G. H. Lewes, John Oxenford, G. A. Sala, and the rest. Whether the success of the *Cornhill* should be attributed to the brilliance of Thackeray as an editor, or the cunning of George Smith as a publisher, no one has ever decided. Perhaps the answer is that a blend of both produced the results. However it may be, the publishers sold 110,000 copies of the first number and the magazine settled down to a steady circulation of 80,000 to 85,000 copies a month.

In the beginning, at any rate, it was largely Thackeray's child. To it he contributed *Lovel the Widower*, *The Four Georges*, and *Philip*, besides writing the *Roundabout Papers* every month. The last were a series of delightful essays in his charming, gossipy style.

He did not remain long in the editorial chair, resigning in 1862. He confessed in a half-pathetic, half-humorous note that people made his life a burden to him by writing to him, and sending MSS. to him, at his private address, although they were told clearly in the magazine not to do so. It is doubtful whether he had the hardness of heart necessary to every editor, which enables him to refuse bad or unsuitable work from friends, who expect it to be published just because they are friends. The successful editor has no friends as far as his magazine is concerned.

By then, also, Thackeray's health was failing, and it had never been perfect. He had told his friend Brookfield when *Vanity Fair* was published that he suffered from a complaint which prevented his insuring his life. Moreover, although he had a good doctor he was not a good patient. He confessed frankly:

"What is the use of advice if you don't follow it? They tell me not to drink, and I do drink. They tell me not to eat, and I do eat. In short, I do everything I am not to do, and, therefore, what is to be expected?"

The expected happened that very year.

Thackeray's was not a long life as we reckon life nowadays, but he had lived hard. One friend of his said to another in the early 1840s that Thackeray wrote half the day, which is a great deal although it may not sound much to people in routine jobs. The friend went on:

"Reviews and newspapers all the morning; dining, drinking, and talking of a night; managing to preserve a fresh colour and perpetual flow of spirits under a wear and tear of thinking and feeding that would have knocked up all the other men I know two years ago at least."

That is the picture of Thackeray at the age of round about thirty, before he had become famous, when he was doing any work he could get.

Nevertheless, he can be called a happy man, except for the tragedy of his wife's mental illness. He liked to live well, and would rather work hard to do it than economise and work less. He wrote at high pressure, mostly in hotels and clubs. He said:

"There is an excitement in public places which sets my brain working." He wrote much at the Athenaeum and the Garrick, though the former could hardly be called an exciting place.

In 1859, four years before his death, he took a lease of an old house at Palace Green, pulled it down, and built in its place a red brick Queen Anne house. He moved there in November, 1862, a year before he died.

On December 12th, 1863, he attended Founder's Day at Charterhouse for the last time. On the evening of December 23rd he worked on the proofs of *Denis Duval*, his last novel, destined to remain unfinished. In the opinion of Sir Leslie Stephen, it gave promise of a return to his old standard, that of *Esmond*. The last words he revised were:

"And my heart throbbed with an exquisite bliss."

Next morning he was found dead in bed from cerebral haemorrhage. He lies buried at Kensal Green.

What is the final verdict on Thackeray and his work? I think we shall not find a better than that of Anthony Trollope, also a gifted novelist, a contemporary, and a shrewd man with both feet on the ground. Trollope wrote in his autobiography, considering the novelists of his day:

"I do not hesitate to name Thackeray the first. His knowledge of human nature was supreme, and his characters stand out as human beings, with a force and truth which has not, I think, been within the reach of any other English novelist in any period. I know no character in fiction, unless it be Don Quixote, with whom the reader becomes so intimately acquainted as with Colonel Newcome. How great a thing it is to be a gentleman at all parts! How we admire the man of whom as much may be said with truth! Is there any one of whom we feel more sure in this respect than of Colonel Newcome? It is not because Colonel Newcome is a perfect gentleman that we think Thackeray's work to have been so excellent, but because he has had the power to describe him as such, and to force us to love him, a weak and silly old man, on account of this grace of character. . . .

"Among all our novelists his style is the purest, as to my ear it is also the most harmonious. Sometimes it is disfigured by a slight touch of affectation, by little concerts which smell of the oil;—but the language is always lucid. The reader, without labour, knows what he means, and knows all that he means . . . I think that any critics examining his work minutely, would find that every scene, and every part of every scene, adds something to the clearness with which the story is told. Among all his stories there is not one which does not leave on the mind a feeling of distress that women should ever be immodest or men dishonest,—and of joy that women should be so devoted and men so honest . . . The hatred of evil and love of good can hardly have come upon so many readers without doing much good."

Thackeray was a great gentleman and a great writer, who lived life to the full and died in harness. He might have said with Walter Savage Landor:

> " *I strove with none, for none was worth my strife,*
> *Nature I loved and after nature art :*
> *I warmed both hands before the fire of life ;*
> *It sinks, and I am ready to depart.*"

CHARLES DICKENS
(1812–1870)

CHARLES DICKENS

From the canvas by Ary Scheffer now in the
National Portrait Gallery

CHARLES DICKENS
(1812–1870)

ONE CANNOT define Charles Dickens; one can only tell his story. He is the great enigma among novelists, and few men have presented such a mass of contradictions. The medical psychologist might be able to explain his singular temperament, but medical psychologists deal in abstractions. In the case of Dickens it is better to let the facts speak for themselves, and leave the reader to draw his own conclusions, if he can.

It seems certain that the whole of Dickens's life was biased by the sordidness of his childhood. This gave him a psychological kink which dominated his work, and the childhood motif appears over and over again. In *Pickwick* he gives us a good man struggling against adversity and at times overwhelmed by it. In *Oliver Twist* we find the picture of a boy wronged from birth, driven by chance into villainous surroundings, struggling through horror and despair to find peace at last. In *Nicholas Nickleby* the same theme recurs, and we meet it again in *The Old Curiosity Shop, Martin Chuzzlewit, Dombey and Son* and *David Copperfield*. His frustrated childhood had become an obsession.

The *Dictionary of National Biography* remarks somewhat dubiously:

"If literary fame could be safely measured by popularity with the half-educated, Dickens must claim the highest position among English novelists." The explanation of his appeal to the half-educated is simple: he was half-educated himself, and it was with the half-educated that he was most familiar. This explanation is not vitiated by the fact that he entered later the charmed circle of Holland House, that he moved eventually in ducal circles, that he won the admiration of Queen Victoria, produced theatrical performances for her special benefit, and was on one occasion received in audience for an hour and a half. It is still true, as the *Dictionary of National Biography* points out, that:

"The criticism of more severe critics chiefly consists in the assertion that his merits are such as suit the half-educated . . . his vivid perception of external oddities passes into something like hallucination." The same authority adds:

"The critic is apt to complain that Dickens kills his children as if he liked it."

There is, to the discerning observer, a certain mental sadism about Dickens. Two continents wept over the death of Little Nell, and no one wept more copiously than Dickens. On the other hand, he became the father of ten children, and exported his sons to the ends of the earth at the earliest opportunity. Dame Una Pope-Hennessy, his latest biographer, claims that his attitude to pregnancy and childbirth, in the case of his wife, was outwardly unsympathetic and often that of a low comedian. He took a morbid interest in prisons and work-houses. He went to see a man hanged and to see an execution by guillotine. Emotionally he appears to have been unstable. He developed extraordinary passions for various women including the youthful Queen Victoria at the time of her marriage. Her Majesty affected him so acutely that he could not work. He wrote to Walter Savage Landor that he had fallen hopelessly in love with her. This was in 1840, four years after his marriage.

Dickens was essentially an extrovert, so that, except while engaged in writing a book, when he worked in a kind of fever, until he had ended the job, he could not bear to be alone. Created to be the life of the party at any party, he won this tribute from Anthony Trollope, another extrovert:

"Of the general charm of his manner I despair of giving any idea to those who have not seen or known him. He warmed the social atmosphere, whenever he appeared, with that summer glow which seemed to attend him. His laugh was brimful of enjoyment."

He neither thought nor read. He was a reporter who reported life, or what he took to be life.

Charles John Huffam Dickens was born in 1812, the second child of his father, John Dickens, and his mother, born Elizabeth Barrow. John Dickens began his working career as a clerk in the Navy Pay Office. By the time he married he earned a salary of £200 a year, which meant the equivalent of at least £400 a year nowadays. At the time of Dickens's birth the family lived at Portsmouth, and he was christened at St. Mary's Church, Portsea.

Unfortunately, John Dickens lacked money sense, and had a habit of getting into debt, for which he was arrested twice, in 1824 and 1834. Dickens has portrayed him in the character of Mr. Micawber. In spite of the fact that his father received a settled income from the Civil Service, Dickens's childhood was dominated by his parents' money troubles and he never knew that sense of security which, psychologists tell us, is indispensable if childhood is to be happy.

In 1814 John Dickens received a transfer to Somerset House, but the year 1817 found him and his family at Chatham. Thus to uncertainty about money was added the lack of a settled home. That uncertainty about money existed must be ascribed purely to John Dickens's temperament. By the time Charles was eight John earned £350 a year, on which he should have been able to keep his family decently if not luxuriously.

Dickens was a small, sickly boy, who showed neither the inclination nor the capacity to play games. Lacking energy, he amused himself by reading everything in his father's small library, which included *Tom Jones*, *The Vicar of Wakefield*, *Gil Blas*, *Robinson Crusoe*, *Don Quixote* and *The Arabian Nights*. These are more remarkable for incident than plot or construction, and, true to his models, the works of Dickens are chiefly works of incident.

He received his earliest education from his mother, but the most solid part of it, such as it was, came from William Giles, son of a Baptist minister, who kept a small school at Chatham. William Giles found Charles a promising pupil, and recommended him to study Goldsmith as a model for English style.

The year 1823 saw John Dickens back at Somerset House, but this time Charles did not remove with the family and remained with William Giles. His parents settled in Camden Town, and his sister Fanny, who had a musical gift, became a pupil at the Royal College of Music, where she achieved success.

From his earliest years he exhibited the explorer's instinct. When he lived at Chatham he explored Rochester, and when, in the spring of 1823, he rejoined his family at Camden Town he examined the neighbourhood minutely. He loved best to explore Seven Dials if he could find anyone to take him there. Though W. S. Gilbert has assured us that:

> " *Hearts just as pure and fair*
> *May beat in Belgrave Square*
> *As in the lowly air*
> *Of Seven Dials,*"

at any rate in Charles Dickens's boyhood the neighbourhood had an unsavoury reputation and atmosphere which fascinated him. He also investigated Soho, where his invalid uncle, Thomas Barrow, lived in Gerrard Street; and Limehouse, where his godfather, Christopher Huffam, after whom he was named, carried on the business of a ship chandler.

Dickens's mind was synthetic, not analytic, and these boyhood wanderings about London and Chatham and Rochester provided him with background and incidents for his novels. A child's mind is plastic, and childhood's impressions remain. He stored up local colour in his child's mind as later in life he might have recorded it on paper.

At this time he was eleven years old, and he had arrived at that period of life the scars of which were to remain with him until he died. He loved books and learning, but when he reached Camden Town there arose no question of his returning to school. Instead he became a family drudge, sharing the housework and blacking the family boots. As it turned out, blacking was to leave its mark on him both physically and psychologically. His father became involved in one of his recurring financial crises. Mrs. Dickens decided to set up a small school, the last refuge of the incompetent, in order to help out the family fortunes, but, in spite of a brass plate on her door, and advertising by means of handbills, she did not ensnare a solitary pupil.

The Dickenses came down to selling some of their possessions and pawning others, and John Dickens seemed on the point of being arrested for debt. At this crisis James Lamert, the son of Mrs. Dickens's sister by a second marriage, offered to take Charles off his family's hands. James, in partnership with a cousin, was running a blacking factory at Hungerford Stairs. He offered Charles a job at seven shillings a week, to the unbounded delight of Mrs. Dickens. Thus Charles celebrated his twelfth birthday.

Now, though many eminent Labour Leaders (so fashionable nowadays) went to work at this age, or even earlier, without any disastrous psychological trauma, the idea of working in a blacking factory seems utterly to have crushed the young Charles. He was a bookish child who longed to learn, and he found himself condemned to a blacking factory, to the utter joy of his parents. These parents he never forgave for their joy.

He has left a detailed picture of the blacking factory, with its rotten floors and staircase, and population of rats. The memory of the degradation he suffered, in his own opinion, by working in a blacking factory, remained with him throughout life. And yet we do not gather that he helped in the manufacture of the loathsome substance, thereby becoming stained both in body and soul. His principal occupation was to stick the labels on the blacking bottles, a boring but not revolting task.

A biographer has explained the reason for his sufferings in these words:

"As a boy he was what he remained all his life through—nervous, highly strung, excitable, profoundly sensitive and imaginative to the last degree, extraordinarily impressionable, and as tenacious in recollecting as he was quick in registering the impressions he received. This boy, so sensitive and shrinking, found himself the sport of fate. The misfortunes of his father were visited on his innocent head with a force increased tenfold by his helplessness and his sense of the injustice of the visitation.

"To be degraded through a father's calamity is the sharpest stroke that can fall upon a boy, for a boy can make no allowances; he can only realise the exceeding bitterness of his own lot. My father, he says in effect, is a grown man; he can fight for himself. But I am made a mockery to my companions by his fall; my days are rendered hateful to me, and I cannot lift a hand to better my condition or to help him.

"So the Marshalsea prisoner's son, forced into an occupation against which his whole being revolted, and of which he could never trust himself in after life to speak, became a lonely and morbid boy. He took refuge in books and the fancies their reading gave him, resolving, too, that if ever the chance came to him after he was grown up he would strike a blow against injustice, oppression, and hypocrisy in high places, and against all the wretchedness and pain that they brought upon gentle and innocent creatures."

To put the situation in a sentence, at the age of twelve Dickens conceived a grudge against the world which he determined to take out on it, if possible, later on. It is a matter of history that he succeeded admirably, though he killed himself in doing so. As Oscar Wilde wrote:

> " *Yet each man kills the thing he loves,*
> *By each let this be heard,*
> *Some do it with a bitter look,*
> *Some with a flattering word,*
> *The coward does it with a kiss,*
> *The brave man with a sword!*"

Dickens certainly loved himself better than he loved anyone else, and he wore himself out at the early age of fifty-eight through deliberate overwork, in spite of being a wealthy man, for he died worth £93,000.

It was on February 7th, 1824, that Charles began work at the blacking factory, and on February 20th his father suffered arrest for debt and imprisonment at the Marshalsea. There he remained until May 28th of that year. Charles found lodgings at first in Camden Town, later south of the river nearer his work. He took breakfast and supper at the prison with his parents, who had no wish for release, because in prison they felt safe from their creditors.

In three months' time John Dickens returned to his job in the Navy Pay Office. He also quarrelled with James Lamert and took Charles away from the blacking factory. Mrs. Dickens wanted him to go back, and Charles remembered this against her to his dying day.

The Navy Pay Office then dismissed John Dickens, on

account of his having taken advantage of the Insolvent Debtor's Act, allowing him a pension of £145 a year. Being only forty, and capable of writing shorthand, he obtained work as parliamentary reporter for a newspaper entitled the *British Press*. Consequently Charles continued his education at a school in Hampstead, which featured theatrical productions and may have given him that bias towards the theatre which he developed so strongly in later life.

During his schooldays at Hampstead an uncle died, leaving £1,300 to be shared between his nephews and nieces. Things began to look up for him.

He left school in the spring of 1827, being then fifteen, and became office boy to a firm of solicitors. He remained there only a few weeks and then became clerk to a second firm of solicitors. In his spare time he studied shorthand, and after eighteen months' studying resigned from the firm of solicitors and became a reporter in the Consistory Court of Doctors' Commons. There he acquired a profound contempt for the Law.

It was now that his extreme thoroughness began to be appreciated. This thoroughness is the outstanding virtue of Charles Dickens. In his reporting days he would rather have killed himself than fail to complete a job. His recreations were the theatre and musical evenings at home with his sister Fanny (of the Royal College of Music) and her friends. He also studied the art of acting with the idea that, if all else failed, he might become an actor. At this period he suffered his first love affair.

Her name was Maria Beadnell; and a friend of Fanny Dickens who admired Charles introduced him to Maria, to whose elder sister this friend had become engaged. The Beadnell family never took Charles seriously because he was young and poor, but he adored Maria. Though she scorned him in the end, she contributed towards his successful career because on account of her he worked harder than ever, since there is nothing so creative as the sex instinct, and no spur to a man like desire for a particular woman.

Maria made the most of Charles until her sister married his friend, and then her parents sent her to school in Paris. At the end of the romance Charles wrote her cruel letters, and

sent back her presents, as many another young man has done
in similar circumstances, at the same time giving her the
satisfying assurance that he could never love any other woman.
Author-like, he used her as copy in two of his novels.

In 1832, at the age of twenty, he joined the staff of an
evening paper and became a reporter in the House of Commons.

At that period politics formed the main interest of the
newspaper reading public, and were taken seriously. It was
before sport had become a religion and its professional prac-
titioners deified. Charles achieved a reputation as a political
reporter very quickly. In the House of Commons Press
Gallery he also saw history unfolding itself, and became
acquainted with public affairs.

On the recommendation of a friend, who described him as
the fastest and most accurate man in the gallery, he obtained
a better position, on the *Morning Chronicle* at a salary of five
guineas a week. When Parliament was not sitting, his work
took him all over the country, for the purpose of reporting
speeches made during the recess, and here his extreme thoroughness counted for a great deal. Since reports could not be tele-
graphed at this period, the news reached London by post-
chaise, and the rivalry between the *Morning Chronicle* and *The
Times* to be first with reports became intense.

In the autumn of 1834 the problem arose in Charles's life
which arises in the lives of all young men beginning to succeed:
the problem of where and how to live. He decided at length
on unfurnished rooms in Furnival's Inn. In the meantime,
like most industrious people with thriftless relations, he found
himself plagued by his parents' money troubles. Out of his
small earnings money needed to be spared for them somehow.
Creditors had once more arrested his father for debt, and
Charles assumed the responsibility for his mother and sisters
and brothers. All this meant a heavy burden for a young man
of twenty-two engaged in an exhausting occupation.

The turning point in his career arrived when, after a year
in the House of Commons, he wrote a sketch called "A Dinner
in Poplar Walk", and submitted it anonymously to the
Monthly Magazine. To his surprise and excitement his con-
tribution was printed. Unfortunately the editor could not
afford to pay his contributors. He could only offer them

publication and a chance of fame. In the summer of 1834 Charles adopted the pen name of "Boz", afterwards to become famous, and his sketches began to appear in his own paper, the *Morning Chronicle*. He wrote these also without payment, but their merit brought the approval of critics, and when the *Evening Chronicle* was born in 1835, his sketches became a feature of the paper, and his salary increased by £2 2s. a week. The sketches are said to have been inspired by the exploits of Mr. Jorrocks, the creation of R. S. Surtees.

Most important of all, Charles now began to make useful friends. Naturally gregarious, and what is now termed a good mixer, he welcomed the entire human race with enthusiasm, particularly those individuals who seemed likely to be useful. He would never have echoed Walter Raleigh's lines, even if they had been written at this period:

> " *I wish I loved the human race ;*
> *I wish I loved its silly face ;*
> *I wish I liked the way it talks ;*
> *I wish I liked the way it walks,*
> *And when I'm introduced to one*
> *I wish I thought* ' What Jolly Fun ! ' "

One of these was Harrison Ainsworth, the writer (1805–1882. Author of novels *Rookwood*, *The Tower of London*, *Windsor Castle*, *The Lancashire Witches*, etc.). He was good-looking, with wavy, windswept hair, and was living apart from his wife with another lady. Like so many writers, Ainsworth loved the society of writers and gave parties for them, including Dickens. Through him Charles met Ainsworth's publisher, Macrone, who said that Charles's sketches ought to be published in book form, and illustrated by George Cruikshank, the celebrated artist. The book duly appeared, entitled *Sketches by Boz*. The *Athenaeum* praised it, and so did John Forster in the *Examiner*. It is to Forster's biography of Charles Dickens that we owe most of our knowledge of him.

That was in 1836, and early in the year another important event took place. Mr. Hall, of Chapman & Hall, the publishers, called on Charles at Furnival's Inn. Charles did not live in any great style at Furnival's Inn. A visiting American author of the period, Nat Willis, has left a picture of his establishment. Mr. Willis, having climbed a long flight of stairs, found himself in an uncarpeted room with a deal table, two or three chairs, a few books, Charles, and a small boy. The boy was his brother Frederick. As the guest entered, Charles took off a ragged writing jacket and put on a blue surtout. These poverty-stricken surroundings arose from the fact that Charles was busy rescuing his family from its money troubles.

The visit of Mr. Hall is historic because it produced the germ of *The Pickwick Papers*. He asked Charles to write a series to be illustrated with sporting sketches. The series was to describe the adventures of a band of sportsmen. Charles loathed the idea and knew nothing of sport, but Mr. Hall offered £14 a month and a royalty on sales, and this sounded too good to be refused.

On the strength of his growing income, and, as he told an uncle, the great success of his new book, *Sketches by Boz*, Charles decided to marry. To him marriage formed part of the picture of a successful young man. Marriage announced to the world that he must be successful, for he could afford to marry. His bride was Catharine Hogarth, better known as Kate, eldest of the daughters of George Hogarth, a friend of Charles, who also worked for the *Morning Chronicle*. George had begotten what today seems the astonishing family of fourteen children, and three of his daughters all looked very much alike. The reason why Charles proposed to Catharine was that the younger Misses Hogarth had not arrived at marriageable age; otherwise, his heart having been broken by Miss Beadnell, any one of them would have suited him as well as another. He longed for marriage rather than any particular girl, or any particular Miss Hogarth.

Catharine was pretty and so were her sisters; Catharine's portrait shows her to have possessed a small, kissable mouth, rather prominent eyes, a chin reminiscent of Queen Victoria's as a young woman, that is retreating and obstinate, and a mass of dark hair. Her personality can only be described as dull, and she suffered from low spirits. Had Charles known that one day he would become a celebrity he might well have chosen someone more suitable. There is no evidence to show that Catharine loved Charles intensely, but the family welcomed him with delight; what parents of fourteen children would not welcome a promising young man eager to take one of their daughters off their hands?

Charles at the period of his engagement was definitely beautiful, far more beautiful than Catharine. As yet clean-shaven, he wore his waving hair in a page's bob, and had begun to burgeon where clothes and ornaments were concerned. He modelled himself on the young Disraeli, and Count d'Orsay, king of the dandies, though the tremendous d'Orsay seems rather a strange model for the smallish Charles. He tended towards the flashy in his dress and liked gold chains and diamond rings on his person and a plenitude of mirrors in his home.

They were married on April 2nd, 1836, at St. Luke's, Chelsea. Two days earlier the first number of *The Pickwick Papers* had appeared. They spent their honeymoon near Rochester, a city beloved of Charles, but on the whole the honeymoon bored him. It lasted for a week, and then they returned to Furnival's Inn, and he began to work on the second number of *Pickwick*.

Of the first number 400 copies were printed. The series achieved no striking success until the fifth number; by the fifteenth number the circulation had increased a hundredfold, and Charles had arrived as an author. Except for the first three numbers the series was illustrated by Hablot K. Browne, a young artist of twenty, who signed his drawings "Phiz". Thus *Pickwick* may be described as a triumph of youth, since the author was only four years older than the artist.

To the author who had arrived, drudgery in the Press Gallery of the House of Commons made no appeal, and Charles decided to give it up. To repair the loss of his salary he made contracts for work in every direction. Macrone contracted in June for a novel to be completed in six months, paying £150 for the copyright. When the Charles Dickenses were on holiday at Petersfield in that wonderful year 1836, Richard Bentley, also a publisher, offered Charles £500 for the copyright of a novel the title, the subject, and the delivery date of which were left completely in the air. Charles agreed, and also to write a second novel on the same terms as the first. With

Macrone's novel that made three, and there is a lot of work in three novels. He also had a farce, *The Strange Gentleman*, and a piece with music called "The Village Coquette" in rehearsal.

In the autumn the Dickenses asked Catharine's sister, Mary Hogarth, aged sixteen, to live with them. Mary inspired the earliest of Charles's strange passions for women other than his wife. Catharine's first baby was almost due, and so Charles took Mary with him wherever he went. On top of all his novel contracts he was now editing *Bentley's Miscellany*, and writing for it as well. His income had reached pleasing proportions and he continued to advance socially. Richard Bentley proposed him for the Garrick Club.

After the birth of a son, the Furnival's Inn rooms became too congested, with Catharine, Mary, Charles, his brother Frederick, and the baby. Therefore they took a large house in Doughty Street. Here Charles wrote *Pickwick* and *Oliver Twist* simultaneously, the latter appearing serially in *Bentley's Miscellany*. He also gave the parties he loved giving.

Unfortunately a shadow hung over the house in Doughty Street. One night, shortly after they had moved there, Mary died suddenly. The blow to Charles was overwhelming; he ceased to be able to write. Catharine had a miscarriage and they departed to the country for a change of scene. The country visit was followed by a trip to the Continent, which gave Charles a taste for foreign travel that he never lost, and in the future was to indulge frequently and successfully. Yet throughout his life he never recovered completely from Mary Hogarth's death.

We come now to the beginning of John Forster's association with Charles Dickens. They met first in the home of the invaluable Harrison Ainsworth, and they were both twenty-five years of age. Forster collected writers as some people collect stamps. Landor, Carlyle, Tennyson, Letitia Elizabeth Landon, and Lady Blessington were among his friends. His fame rests on his biography of Dickens, though at least one critic complains that in this work the biographer is almost as prominent as his subject. Forster (1812–1876) was the eldest son of a Newcastle cattle-dealer, and was educated for the Bar, but devoted himself to writing for periodicals. His

political articles in the London *Examiner* brought him a repu-
ation. He edited successfully the *Foreign Quarterly Review, Daily
News,* and *Examiner,* and ended his career as a Commissioner
n Lunacy.

From the beginning of the friendship Forster practically
absorbed Charles, who had the deepest admiration for his
business capabilities, ignoring Catharine, and behaving with
suspicion towards Charles's friends. Never did the man and
he hour coincide more auspiciously. When he met Forster,
Charles, like so many novelists, was in trouble over his contracts.
He was involved in novel contracts with Macrone, Bentley,
and Chapman & Hall. He was writing *Pickwick* and *Oliver
Twist* and editing *Bentley's Miscellany.* No human being could
cope with all this work. Charles began to feel like a rat in a
trap. If only he could get rid of Macrone's novel, at least!

Finally he gave up all rights in *Sketches by Boz* in return for
being released from his contract to write Macrone's novel.
Then Macrone decided to issue the Sketches in green paper
covers in imitation of *Pickwick,* which was now selling 40,000
copies a month. Charles persuaded Chapman & Hall to
take over the copyright of the Sketches for a payment to
Macrone of £2,000, which Charles was to guarantee, the
security being the profits on *Pickwick* for five years. He was
also to write another book to be issued in twenty monthly
instalments at £150 a month.

His next exploit was to quarrel with Bentley. What he
could never understand was that a contract is a contract, no
matter how much the author's value may rise after the contract
is made. He could not bear to think that a few months after
he had sold the copyright of *Barnaby Rudge* for three years to
Bentley for £700, Chapman & Hall were paying him £3,000
for the copyright of *Nicholas Nickleby* for five years. It seemed
to him that Bentley must obviously be robbing him. He did
not take the rapid rise in his popularity as an author into
consideration.

Consequently he decided that he could not continue to
work for Bentley, and explained this to Forster. He resigned
the editorship of the *Miscellany* and Harrison Ainsworth reigned
over it in his stead. Forster arranged with Chapman & Hall
to buy all rights in *Oliver Twist* for £2,500 from Bentley, who

would also relinquish the *Barnaby Rudge* contract. Charles now had all his eggs in Chapman & Hall's basket.

There are two sides to every question, and in the matter of Charles's quarrel with Bentley, part of a letter which appeared in the *Times Literary Supplement* dated March 2nd, 1946, deserves quotation:

"This question (the relations between Dickens and Bentley) may well be disputed for years to come by the experts, of whom I am not one; but it ought to be known that there is one substantial body of evidence, crucial to the controversy, which remains unpublished, and has never, I believe, been fully drawn upon. This is the collection of Dickens's original letters to Bentley, copies of the replies, the publisher's copies of various contracts and agreements, and other cognate documents, which were preserved after the demise of the firm in 1898, by the late Mr. Richard Bentley.

"This collection, which contains over one hundred unpublished letters (the majority dating from 1837–1840), is now in the possession of Messrs. Scribners of New York; and my colleague, Mr. David Randall, who has made a thorough study of its contents, is of the opinion that when the letters are eventually edited and published they will confirm that Forster's account of the matter was in many respects decidedly unfair to Bentley.

"I may perhaps quote as an example of the case for the defence, George Bentley's endorsement on one long letter from Dickens to his lawyers, attacking the firm and expounding his view that Bentley's alleged behaviour released him from his *Barnaby Rudge* contract.

" 'The charges made in this letter,' he wrote, 'are false. I do not, however, destroy the letter. It is a brick in the building up of Dickens's character. He wished to break his agreement and so he made up the account contained herein. Dickens was a very clever but he was not an honest man. George Bentley.'

"(Signed) John Carter."

We have now followed Charles in his career to the point where money worries had become a thing of the past. Though occasionally he felt it necessary to economise because he loved spending and sometimes overspent, he never again found himself short of money, for the economies arose rather from precaution than necessity, and he died a rich man in spite of his family of ten children. It is impossible in a 12,000-word sketch to include every detail of his career, because his interests were widespread and his energy, until the last phase, inexhaustible. A point which needs emphasising is that he worked like a slave, and that, if ever a man deserved to become rich, he deserved to.

All his novels appeared in twenty instalments and were about 350,000 words long, with the exception of three. The average 8s. 6d. novel of today is about 80,000 words long. Sometimes, as in the case of *Pickwick* and *Oliver Twist*, he wrote two simultaneously, adding to each in turn. If he was writing only one he would work desperately for a fortnight and then rest.

A successful novelist can, if he chooses, cut a prominent figure in what is, or used to be, called society, and at the age of twenty-six Charles began to cut such a figure. Twenty-six is not such a great age, and seeing that he had earned the opportunity by intense industry, we can hardly blame him, if that sort of thing appealed to him.

It was now that the small Charles began to imitate Count d'Orsay, who was six feet four inches tall. What Mr. Salteena in Daisy Ashworth's *The Young Visiters* called "a little gaierty" established itself in his waistcoats and he indulged his weakness for jewellery. He wore his frock coats supremely waisted. Celebrated artists took his portrait, and women fell for him in heaps.

He became the friend of men like Monckton Milnes, Walter Savage Landor, and Samuel Rogers. He was seen in the scented gloom of Lady Blessington's drawing-room at Gore House, and at Lady Holland's intellectual junkets at Holland House. Mr. Rogers gave breakfasts, and among the guests whom Charles would meet appeared Macaulay, Mrs. Norton, and the Chatelaine of Gore House.

It was Serjeant Talfourd who introduced Charles into Gore House and Holland House. Lady Holland asked Bulwer privately whether Charles was fit to be seen under her roof, and, on being reassured, invited him and described him, somewhat lukewarmly, as modest and well-behaved. However, she harboured no illusions about his style. She called it "his Pickwick style" and wrote thus to a friend concerning *The Chimes*:

"Dickens's Xmas book I full intended sending you today, but it is such a failure that I cannot finish it myself. So how would you, who do not relish Dickens, endure it?"

The Misses Berry lured him to their small, select, crowded *salon*, whose success Agnes Berry attributed in part to her wonderful flair for arranging sofas and chairs, and thus he became linked faintly and indirectly with Horace Walpole. In 1838 he was elected to the Athenæum Club, the holy of holies of Clubland.

In all these goings-on Catharine Dickens played no part. Her simple, cow-like personality would have failed entirely to attract the glittering mentalities of Gore House, Holland House, and Samuel Roger's abode in St. James's Place.

Neither did Charles's family chime with his new exaltation, and so they became what are known nowadays as evacuees. He took a house for his parents in Devonshire, which is a long way from London, furnished it, and installed the family within a week. Forster was involved in all this. Forster was now a sort of manager for Charles. It all had to be very secret because his parents, as usual, were in debt. At first they complained, as all sponging parents do, but eventually they settled down.

Charles arranged with Chapman & Hall for a threepenny weekly, called, of all things, *Master Humphrey's Clock*, on magazine lines. For this he wanted £50 a week, the profits to be shared equally. Generously enough, Chapman & Hall consented. Catharine was having a baby as usual. They wanted a house with a garden for the children, and so Charles took one in Devonshire Terrace. He furnished it lavishly. Why not, since he was rich?

In 1841 he decided to visit the United States. Amazingly enough, he decided also to take Catharine, who never received invitations from his influential friends in England, with him. The house was let, the four children were boarded out, and Catharine, with many tears, for she hated and feared foreign travel, provided herself with clothes suitable to any American emergency, however exalted. Charles, too, dressed the part, launching out into more frock coats, the coloured waistcoats he adored, and more jewellery.

They landed at Halifax, Nova Scotia, to encounter a welcome from the Speaker of the Legislative Assembly and his wife, and cheering crowds in the streets. In January, 1842, they reached Boston and Charles went ashore in a beaver hat, a brown frock coat, a waistcoat of red, and a large scarf controlled by two diamond pins linked by a chain, thus anticipating the glories of Hollywood film stars yet unborn.

The flood of invitations obliged him to engage a secretary. They had landed on a Saturday, and attended church on the following Sunday, and by Monday the welcome had reached a pitch of hysteria only equalled nowadays by devotees of a visiting film favourite. The leading personalities of Boston offered Charles a banquet, and his speech won loud applause, until he referred to the question of international copyright. All his books, he explained, had been pirated in the United States, and so had Sir Walter Scott's. He demanded an international arrangement respecting copyright.

This matter of copyright had festered in his bosom for a long time, and no one can withhold sympathy, because the pirating of his books abroad caused him to lose large sums of money. In 1837 he had discussed with Serjeant Talfourd the terms of Talfourd's Copyright Bill, which endeavoured to protect an author's rights in his work for sixty years. In the matter of piracy the London publishers of those days were not much better than those of France and the United States. Talfourd's Bill did not become law, and it remained for the Literary Copyright Act of 1842 to protect the copyright of authors in England. The rights of British subjects abroad are protected today by the Berne Convention of 1886, and additional Acts, Conventions and Protocols of 1896, 1908, and 1914.

Authors and citizens of the countries embraced by the Copyright Union enjoy the rights which the laws of the respective countries give to natives. The United States is not a member of the Copyright Union. An English book to be copyright in the United States must be "entirely manufactured within

United States territory", though an *ad interim* copyright may be obtained by depositing copies of the English edition at the Library of Washington and the payment of a fee.

Charles's remarks on copyright at the Boston banquet were entirely ignored by native speakers. Having, by his want of tact, forfeited American sympathy, he took a dislike to the United States, and wrote home contemptuous letters about American institutions. Nevertheless, the warmth of the Boston welcome continued until, in a fortnight, he had reached a state of collapse, and Catharine wept more copiously than usual. There is some excuse for their exhaustion. During their tour of the country they were obliged to shake hands with from two hundred to seven hundred people in a single day.

Having learned nothing from his experience at Boston, Charles referred once more to the question of copyright at a banquet at Hartford, to find his remarks received in a similar icy silence. The local press, on the other hand, told him plainly to hold his tongue on the subject. As the tour continued he began to feel the strain of living perpetually in a fierce glare of publicity. He found it a relief to arrive in Canada, where the Coldstream Guards persuaded him to take part in their amateur theatricals at Montreal. Nothing could have pleased him better, in view of his passion for the theatre.

In June 1842 Charles and Catharine returned to England. Their American tour had not proved an unmitigated success, but in spite of contention over copyright the memory of American adulation lingered.

Charles and Catharine collected their four children and took up life again at Devonshire Terrace. To the family circle they now added Georgina Hogarth, Catharine's little sister. She resembled greatly Charles's lost playmate, the late Mary Hogarth. She is important in the story of Charles, and will recur later.

Like many other people, he did not gain much benefit from his first visit to the United States, for that great country requires a second visit in order to be appreciated and understood. He wrote on his return a book entitled *American Notes* which was unremarkable, but it sold and made money, and he needed money because American travel is costly. He then began a new novel, finally to be known as *Martin Chuzzlewit*, which appeared, like his previous works, in twenty monthly issues. It contained lampoons of American characters and customs. A copy was destroyed on the stage in New York amid loud cheers. Charles, of course, had no American sales to worry about since his books were pirated in the United States.

Martin Chuzzlewit occupied most of the year 1843. However, in this year also he conceived the idea of *A Christmas Carol* which, containing as it does the characters Ebenezer Scrooge, Tiny Tim, and Bob Cratchit, has survived as an all-time weepie. He wrote it in a month, and Chapman & Hall published it. He only received £500 for it, a fact which did not improve his relations with his publishers.

Worse still, *Martin Chuzzlewit* sold badly. Chapman & Hall complained, and Charles, repairing to Forster, his philosopher-guide, relieved his feelings about Chapman & Hall. The climax of his fury arrived when Chapman & Hall, as his contract with them permitted, reduced the amount they paid him monthly, to cover advances made to him during the previous year. He wished to break off relations, but Forster calmed him. Later in the year, however, he transferred to another firm, Messrs. Bradbury & Evans. It is characteristic of authors that when their affairs are going well they take credit to themselves, and when things are going badly they blame their publishers. Unfortunately these quarrels and crises always drove Charles to the limit of nervous excitement.

For the sake of economy he decided now to spend a year abroad, this measure being a stock remedy in the nineteenth century for a depleted bank balance. The house in Devonshire Terrace was let, and another taken in Italy, and Charles began to learn Italian. The *Morning Chronicle* refused to pay the price he demanded for contributions from Italy, and he shook the dust of its office from his feet, and laid plans for starting a rival paper in revenge. The admirable Forster lent his guidance in this matter. Charles bought a travelling carriage wherein to traverse the Continent, which, as he recorded, required four horses to draw it, the horses wearing between them ninety-six bells.

They travelled through France to Italy, sometimes conveying the coach by water, and finally reached Albaro, their destination, and the Villa Bella Vista, their new home, to which they took immediately a violent dislike. All the domestic shortcomings of the Villa he left entirely to his wife. As Somerset Maugham has said, the artist requires his comforts; he should not inhabit a villa in Brixton and consume toad-in-the-hole prepared by a general servant. The same theory applied no doubt to a villa in Italy.

In the end the Villa Bella Vista became too much even for a domestic woman of Catharine's cow-like temperament, and so the Dickenses moved to a palace in Genoa, and there they became acquainted with a Mr. and Mrs. De la Rue. Mrs. De la Rue was English and her husband Swiss. Mrs. De la Rue, who suffered from delusions, took a fancy for Charles, and became in due time one of the female crushes with which his life seemed doomed to be dotted. Charles had long ago dabbled in hypnotism, and proposed, with the approval of Mr. De la Rue, to exorcise the demons which pursued Mrs. De la Rue. We can understand Mr. De la Rue's attitude, for nothing could be more boring than a wife haunted by demons. Sometimes Mrs. De la Rue developed a psycho-pathological crisis in the middle of the night, when Charles would arise to deal with it.

For the first time in her married life Catharine found herself shaken. She had endured Charles's moon-struck condition over her sister Mary, and this episode ended with Mary's sudden death. She could pass over his companionship with her sister Georgina. But a haunted Swiss banker's wife who called Charles from his marital bed in the middle of the night because she found herself tied up in knots seemed rather too much to endure.

However, in Genoa he conceived the idea for *The Chimes*, of which we have already noted Lady Holland's opinion. Charles considered it greatly superior to *A Christmas Carol*. Thanks to the influence of Mrs. De la Rue, it was full of goblins. It appeared as the Christmas book of 1844 and brought him £1,500, so there was something to be said for goblins, and even, perhaps, the goblin-haunted Mrs. De la Rue. Lady Blessington adored it. Charles Brookfield said it was as utter trash as was ever trodden underfoot.

At Rome, on his way to England, he saw the execution by guillotine referred to earlier. He noted that the head of the victim—a young man—rolled instantly into a leather bag, there was a great deal of blood, and the scaffold was very dirty.

The fruit of his Italian wanderings came in the shape of a volume *Pictures from Italy*, published by Bradbury & Evans. At last the moment arrived to pack and return home. Being a typical Victorian husband, he left the drudgery of packing to Catharine and went visiting. The family reached their London home in safety after a year abroad, their financial position now thoroughly sound.

Catharine bore her sixth child, a boy, in October 1845, and Charles, appalled by the number of his children, cast about very prudently for a means of making more money. Although in the second half of the nineteenth century income tax was from sixpence to eightpence in the pound, the expense of a wife and six children cannot in any circumstances appear trifling. Apart from writing *The Cricket on the Hearth* as a Christmas story, he contemplated founding a newspaper in the Liberal interest, a plan which gave birth eventually to the *Daily News*, forerunner of the present *News Chronicle*.

The *Daily News* project proved one of the most astonishing episodes of Charles's career. At first he flung himself into the necessary planning with all the nervous energy which made him so dynamic, consulting with backers, engaging staff, flitting from wild enthusiasm at one moment to the depths of despair the next. Messrs. Bradbury & Evans, who were providing capital, found these psychological fluctuations most trying. The staff became distinctly a family affair. His father returned from exile in the west to control the reporters, his father-in-law became musical critic, and an uncle a sub-editor. The *Daily News*, which was to rival *The Times*, was to cost 5*d.* against *The Times's* 7*d.*

The first number of the *Daily News* appeared on January 21st, 1846. Dickens's connection with it may be summed up in the words of a critic:

"He had not the necessary qualifications for the function of editor of a political organ."

Whether he felt this himself cannot be established, but he tired almost immediately of the *Daily News*. He told Forster that he wanted to leave the paper and go abroad to write a new book in shilling numbers. This period may be defined as the restless period of Charles's life. He resigned the editorship on February 9th, 1846, after a reign of nineteen days. Forster replaced him as editor, and Charles's only further connection with the paper was as a contributor of some travel letters about Italy, and some articles on capital punishment, of which, having seen a hanging and a guillotining, he proceeded to disapprove. He let the house in Devonshire Terrace once more, and departed with his family to Lausanne. Catharine had declined to return to Genoa on account of Mrs. De la Rue and her goblins, who still inhabited that city.

At Lausanne, in a room with a view, he began to write *Dombey and Son*, which continued peacefully until in September (1846) he put it aside to write a new Christmas story called *The Battle of Life*, all about a girl who gives up her lover to her sister. In November nostalgia for city streets overwhelmed him. He could not finish his book without city streets to walk in, and crowds about him, and so the Dickens family left Lausanne for Paris, where they took a house for the winter. It belonged to the Marquis de Castellane and Charles described it as a Paris mansion in miniature, with a courtyard, garden, and porter's lodge.

Finding that he could not write in the mansion—the atmosphere was wrong—he paid a visit to London, returned to Paris, and entered on such a glittering social round, full of noble Lords, that *Dombey and Son* hung fire. When Charles eventually killed Paul Dombey he had to refuse an invitation to a masked ball in order to do so, and having committed the murder at ten p.m. on a Friday night felt quite unable to sleep and walked about the streets of Paris until breakfast time.

During the Paris sojourn Catharine was going to have a baby, and so Georgina accompanied Charles on his various expeditions. The baby being due in April 1847, the family returned to London in March and took a house in Chester Place, their own being let, when Catharine bore her fifth son.

They returned to Devonshire Place in the autumn of 1847. Charles was still writing *Dombey and Son*. During the succeeding year he indulged in his favourite hobby of theatricals, and organised performances of *The Merry Wives of Windsor* at the Haymarket Theatre in aid of a curatorship for the Shakespeare House at Stratford-on-Avon. It was a rambling dissatisfied period of his life and we must hasten on. He wrote a Christmas book, *The Haunted Man*, and began *David Copperfield* on the last day of 1847, being then at Norwich, because Catharine was going to have a baby. She bore Henry Fielding Dickens on January 13th, 1848.

For a long time previous to this date he had turned over in his mind the idea of finding some permanent means of putting forward his views on every subject under the sun, in a form which would enter the homes of the people. This scheme resulted, on March 30th, 1850, in the publication of the first number of *Household Words*, a weekly publication edited by himself. To this George Meredith contributed in his youth, and Adelaide Ann Procter, authoress of *The Lost Chord* and *Cleansing Fires*, consigned thither her lugubrious verses. The first number contained the opening instalment of a serial by Mrs. Gaskell, having the delirious title of *Lizzie Lee*. Few would care to read *Household Words* nowadays. but its birth was greeted with enthusiasm. It became a champion of lost causes, producing missionary articles on such subjects as education and the care of paupers. All this succeeded, and Charles had begun a career of twenty years as an editor.

In August of that year Catharine had another baby, and he sent his children to Broadstairs in charge of Georgina, whom he joined after the baby was born, though his wife stayed on at Devonshire Terrace. This is significant in view of what was to happen seven years later.

Also in 1850 Charles combined with Bulwer Lytton to found the Guild of Literature and Art, through which painters and writers who had fallen on evil days could be helped. They planned to raise money for the Guild by giving theatrical performances, the first of which took place at Lytton's home, Knebworth. The scene then changed to London. The bright idea was evolved of giving a performance at the house of one of The Great, and, if possible, interesting Queen Victoria. The Duke of Devonshire kindly agreed to lend his house. Charles's social career now reached its apex, for it became his duty to inquire when it would be convenient for Her Majesty to attend the first performance. The date had to be changed owing to the deaths of his father and his infant daughter, Dora, being fixed finally for May 16th, 1857. The play was *Not So Bad As We Seem*, produced by Charles, who also acted in it.

Queen Victoria, on this occasion, was amused, and applauded graciously, but during the performance Charles showed his first recorded signs of illness since his childhood. The emotion caused by the death of his father and baby, and the excitement of producing the play, brought on swelling in his legs during the first performance, in spite of which he continued to play his part. A tour of the provinces succeeded the London performances, and Charles received ovations accorded nowadays only to popular film stars. By these means he raised £4,000 for the Guild. It all formed part and parcel of his restless energy, which in time was to wear him out.

In 1851 he had removed his family from Devonshire Terrace to Tavistock House, Bloomsbury. This house became the scene of pilgrimages by his admirers from all over the world. Once here, he began to write *Bleak House*, in which he portrayed Leigh Hunt as Harold Skimpole, to the annoyance of that writer. In this year also Catharine took to her pen while in an interesting condition. She wrote a cookery book called *What Shall We Have for Dinner?*, a most excellent title, posing as a certain Lady Maria Clutterbuck. She catered for parties of from two to eighteen covers and Messrs. Bradbury & Evans, who put out her husband's works, published hers.

Her menus create a certain wistfulness in the reader in these starvation times (1946). For a dinner for six to ten people she prescribes soup, two kinds of fish, stewed kidneys, roast lamb, boiled turkey, ham, two kinds of potatoes and stewed onions, cabinet pudding, blancmange and cream, and macaroni.

Catharine then bore her tenth and last child.

The year 1854 saw Charles writing *Hard Times*, which is all about economic doctrines and revolves around a place called Coketown. Also in that year England and France embarked upon the Crimean War against Russia. The Dickens family spent the summer at Boulogne, and here Charles finished *Hard Times*. At Christmas of that year a ghost from the past reincarnated itself in the shape of Maria Beadnell, his first and, as he told her at the time, his only love. He received a letter from her; all his former emotions revived, even though Maria was now Mrs. Winter.

As all wise men know, it is quite fatal to meet the lost love of one's youth, after a long interval, in her middle age, but in this instance Charles was not wise. He caused Catharine to call on Maria, and ask her husband and her to dine at Tavistock House. The result was most unsatisfactory. Maria suspected the truth: Charles, in a letter, wrote nothing to comfort her. Even the lost loves of youth are not proof against Time.

At this period he took the opportunity, while travelling, to look over Gad's Hill, the house near Rochester which he had admired as a boy and longed to live in. Well, he was rich now. He would buy Gad's Hill as soon as possible.

The restless phase continued, and in the autumn of 1855 he decided to go abroad once more, crossed to Paris with Georgina to find an apartment, chose one looking on the Champs Élysées, and for once, with Georgina's help, made the place ready for Catharine and the children instead of leaving this work to Catharine and gallivanting with Georgina. Life then became very social. *Household Words* took him to London once a month, and at last he was able to complete the purchase of Gad's Hill, though he could not take possession until 1857. Back in Paris, he worked on *Little Dorrit* of which 40,000 copies of each number were being sold. He also sat for his portrait; life had scarcely an idle moment, and sitting for the portrait interfered with work on the book. The odour and gold of Paris were exchanged for the seaside air of Boulogne, and then an epidemic sent Charles and family hurrying back to Tavistock House.

There he plunged into rehearsals of a play called *The Frozen Deep*, written by Wilkie Collins in collaboration with Charles. Collins was now his intimate friend, had shared in the Paris and Boulogne excursion, and had become assistant editor of *Household Words*. The main point of interest attaching to this production is that Charles grew a beard for it, in order to look like his idea of a seafarer in northern latitudes, and decided to retain the beard for the rest of his life. Therefore, from this year 1856 onward, he must be visualised as the bearded figure whom we see in his later portraits.

The year 1857 is a landmark in his life. In February of that year he took possession of Gad's Hill. Later in the year arose the circumstances which led to his separation from Catharine in 1858.

In the summer of 1857 he agreed to produce *The Frozen Deep* at Manchester, and among the professional cast he engaged a Mrs. Ternan and her daughters, Maria and Ellen. It was Ellen Lawless Ternan who tempted Charles's wayward heart away from his wife Catharine.

Ellen was a blue-eyed blonde, who took up the attitude towards Charles adopted so successfully towards so many prosperous men by so many young ladies, that he was a great, big, wonderful man. She charmed him particularly because she was so modest. Charles became more and more infatuated, and began, in the classic fashion, to give Ellen jewellery. Catharine discovered this, and her daughters considered her to be badly treated.

Charles ran away from his fate for a time and made an excursion to Carlisle with Wilkie Collins. But escape there was none. He had discovered that while Catharine had become dowdy and middle-aged—not that she had ever shown the wit and charm proper in the wife of such a man as he, he could attract a delicious blue-eyed blonde of eighteen. Obviously he must blame the whole thing on Catharine. He wrote to Forster:

"Poor Catharine and I are not made for each other, and there is no help for it. It is not only that she makes me uneasy and unhappy, but that I make her so, too—and much more so. She is exactly what you know, in the way of being amiable and complying, but we are strangely ill-assorted for the bond there is between us. God knows she would have been a thousand times happier if she had married another kind of man, and that her avoidance of this destiny would have been at least equally good for us both. . . .

"Her temperament will not go with mine. It mattered not so much when we had only ourselves to consider, but reasons have been growing since which make it all but hopeless that we should even try to struggle on."

The reason had been growing for eighteen years, and had blonde hair and blue eyes, and her name was Ellen Lawless Ternan.

Now the children Catharine had borne Charles were:

Charles (born 1837); Mary (born 1838); Kate (born 1839); Walter Landor (born 1841); Francis Jeffrey (born 1843); Alfred Tennyson D'Orsay (born 1845); Sydney Smith Haldemand (born 1847); Henry Fielding (born 1849); Dora Annie (born 1850); Edward Bulwer Lytton (born 1852).

It will be seen that Charles named many of his children after his friends; the most unfortunate was poor Alfred Tennyson D'Orsay, named after two, Alfred Tennyson the poet and Count D'Orsay the king of the dandies.

Forster, a monument of tact, wrote thus in his biography of Charles's and Catharine's separation:

"It was thus far an arrangement of a strictly private nature, and no decent person could have had excuse for regarding it in any other light, if public attention had not been unexpectedly invited to it by a printed statement in *Household Words*. Dickens was stung into this by some miserable gossip at which in ordinary circumstances no man would have more determinedly been silent; but he had now publicly to show himself, at stated times, as a public entertainer, and this, with his name even so aspersed, he found to be impossible. All he could concede to my strenuous resistance against such a publication (in *Household Words*) was an offer to suppress it, if, upon reference to the opinion of a certain distinguished man (still living), that opinion should prove to be in agreement with mine. Unhappily it fell in with his own, and the publication went on. . . .

"The course taken by the author of this book (Forster) at the time of these occurrences, will not be departed from here. Such illustrations of grave defects in Dickens's character as this passage in his life affords, I have not shrunk from placing side by side with such excuses in regard to it as he had unquestionable right to claim should be put forward also. How far what remained of his story took tone or colour from it, and especially from the altered career on which at the same time he entered, will thus be sufficiently explained; and with anything else the public have nothing to do."

Carlyle wrote contractedly and breezily to Emerson on the matter of the separation:

"Fact of separation I believe is true, but all the rest is mere lies and nonsense. No crime and no misdemeanour specifiable

on either side; *unhappy* these two, good many years past, and
they at length end it."

On all the evidence, which is too long to give here, Charles
does not come out of the separation episode very well. He was
concerned at all costs to keep Ellen Ternan out of public
knowledge, and so he put the blame on his wife. He tried to
spare Georgina, who remained with him, any scandal by
stating that except for her the separation would have happened
long ago. He said that Catharine had thankfully agreed to his
terms. All this was set out in a statement which appeared first
in the *New York Times*, later in the English papers.

When they separated after twenty-two years of married
life Charles was forty-six and Catharine forty-three. Charles
junior, the eldest child, an old Etonian, did the Decent Thing,
and went to live with his mother when she retreated to a house
in Gloucester Crescent, Camden Town. Charles had settled
£600 a year on her, an adequate sum in those days for a woman
living alone, though she would not be able to equal the
splendours of Tavistock House or Devonshire Terrace; still
less those of Gad's Hill. The rest, except Dora Annie who
was dead, and Walter Landor who had been exported to India,
remained with Charles and Georgina. Henceforward she was
'to, act as Charles's housekeeper and superintend her nephews
and nieces.

It is noticeable that Georgina did not side with her sister
Catharine.

Charles, who had already given public readings of his works
for charity, now began to read in public for profit. It is to this
project which Forster referred when in the passage quoted
from his biography he wrote:

"He had now publicly to show himself, at stated times, as a
public entertainer." Privately Forster considered these readings rather low, but Charles insisted. Reading was profitable,
and indulged his passion for theatricalism at the same time.
Therefore he condensed scenes from his novels and gave
sixteen readings in London, and then toured the provinces,
Scotland and Ireland. Without knowing it, he had probably
signed his death warrant by becoming a public reader. He
resembled somewhat a theatrical star, for his manager, Arthur
Smith, arranged all the bookings and details.

Kate, his daughter, has left it on record that her father's association with Ellen Ternan and the son she bore him was tragic and far-reaching. He was, she declared, like a madman. Charles had set her up in a house, and Georgina received her at Gad's Hill. The Dickens family certainly had become very queer when Georgina could receive her brother-in-law's mistress as a matter of course.

However, Charles was set on renewing his youth, and cheating Time, which is impossible. He gave up his old men friends and consorted with men younger than himself. He also dyed his hair and beard and burned all the letters he had received from his old friends, and Catharine's with them. He had determined to break with the past and begin life anew, a course which is difficult and unprofitable at the age of forty-six. There is more past than future at that time unless one is prepared to survive beyond the age of ninety-two.

Perhaps it was this passion to break with everything which drove him to quarrel with Messrs. Bradbury & Evans. In 1859 he dissolved his partnership with them in *Household Words*, and bought the stock and the plates, and the right to use the name, at an auction held under a Court order. He then launched a weekly of similar appearance called *All the Year Round*. At the same time he declined to write more novels for Bradbury & Evans, and transferred his novels to his old publishers, Chapman & Hall.

In the autumn of the same year Tavistock House was sold, and he decided to settle at Gad's Hill. He had already planned a tour of "readings" in the United States.

Charles's first serious signs of decay were observed in the spring of 1866, when he complained of pain in one leg, and the doctors diagnosed an irritable heart. Nevertheless he started on a long reading tour. It should be remembered that he acted every character in these readings, a proceeding which subjected him to great nervous strain.

He began the American tour in November, 1867. Forster, realising the state of Charles's health, begged him not to undertake it, but he had been guaranteed £10,000 and the money tempted him. The tour opened in Boston, and he declared that his success could not be greater. The exchange stood then at seven dollars to the pound, and the profits were remarkable.

But he only endured the strain of this tour with the help of cream and rum on waking, a pint of champagne at three p.m., an egg beaten up in sherry before he started reading, and beef tea during the course of it. At a dinner given him in New York City shortly before he sailed for England, he kept the company waiting, and when he arrived he was seen to be so lame he could scarcely walk.

However, the doctor seemed pleased with him when he reached England, and he began another series of readings (1868). Also his son Edward Bulwer Lytton was exported to Australia, where his brother Alfred Tennyson had arrived already. During the tour of readings Charles suffered further symptoms of illness, and was obliged to give up reading and return to Gad's Hill. Early in 1870 he began his last book, which he was never to finish: *The Mystery of Edwin Drood*. He had also contracted for a further series of twelve readings, to begin on January 11th and end on March 15th. The twelfth reading was his last. There followed his reception by Queen Victoria in an audience lasting an hour and a half.

The end came at Gad's Hill. He was dining alone with Georgina when he suffered a stroke which proved fatal. They buried him in Westminster Abbey with the extreme simplicity which he had desired.

So this feverish, exultant life closed peacefully, for, after being struck, he never recovered consciousness. He had loved every moment of it, and had worn himself out at what is now considered the early age of fifty-eight.

The exhausting life had brought its compensations, for he died worth £93,000. His will provides an apposite commentary on his life. He left:

£1,000 free of legacy duty to Miss Ellen Lawless Ternan.

To Georgina Hogarth £8,000 free of legacy duty, all his personal jewellery not hereinafter mentioned, all the little familiar objects from his writing-table and his room. Also all his private papers whatsoever and wheresoever, and "I leave her my grateful blessing as the best and truest friend man ever had".

£8,000 on trust to invest the same to his sons Charles and

Henry Fielding, and to pay the annual income to his wife during her life.

Georgina Hogarth and John Forster to be executrix and executor of his will and guardians of the persons of his children during their respective minorities.

Lastly, he enjoined his dear children always to remember how much they owe to the said Georgina Hogarth, "for they know well that she has been, through all the stages of their growth and progress, their ever-useful, self-denying, and devoted friend".

He desired to record that his wife, since their separation by consent, has received £600 a year from him, "while all the great charges of a numerous and expensive family have devolved solely upon myself".

There follow directions for a simple funeral, which were carried out faithfully, in spite of the Westminster Abbey burial.

Here we leave one of the most enigmatic personalities of the literary or any other world. With Charles Dickens it is a case of so many men, so many minds. He is certainly not an author for the sophisticated, for his novels lack form and style, and his orgies of sentimentality border on the fantastic.

George Lewes recorded that he was more impressed with Dickens's fullness of life and energy than with any sense of distinction. Thackeray praised *David Copperfield*, declaring it superior to his own *Pendennis*. Clifford Bax, in *Evenings in Albany*, discussing Victorian writers, remarked:

"Dickens had, it seems, a gift of immortality which must always puzzle the judicious."

Perhaps the explanation of his vogue is that the vast majority of the electorate are, and probably always will be, simple-minded and childlike, longing to be told a story, careless of style, or taste, or the manner of telling the story. Charles Dickens told them story after story packed with incident, and so they read him and many continue to read him.

If any fanatical admirer of Dickens feels that this sketch has done Dickens less than justice let Anthony Trollope (q.v.) provide the epilogue. He was a contemporary of Dickens, a novelist, and a "sound" person; for he earned part of his living as a civil servant, and hunted, and what could be more sound than that? He wrote of Dickens:

"I do acknowledge that Mrs. Gamp, Micawber, Pecksniff, and the others have become household words in every house, as though they were human beings; but to my judgment they are not human beings, nor are any of the characters human which Dickens has portrayed. It has been the peculiarity and the marvel of this man's power that he has invested his puppets with a charm that has enabled him to dispense with human nature. . . .

"Nor is the pathos of Dickens human. It is stagey and melodramatic. But it is so expressed that it touches every heart a little. There is no real life in Smike. His misery, his idiocy, his devotion for Nicholas, his love for Kate, are all overdone and incompatible with each other. But still the reader sheds a tear. . . .

"Of Dickens's style it is impossible to speak in praise. It is jerky, ungrammatical, and created by himself in defiance of rules—almost as completely as that created by Carlyle. To readers who have taught themselves to regard language, it must therefore be unpleasant. But the critic is driven to feel the weakness of his criticism when he acknowledges to himself— as he is compelled in all honesty to do that with the language, such as it is, the writer has satisfied the great mass of the readers of his country. Both these great writers have satisfied the readers of their own pages; but both have done infinite harm by creating a school of imitators. No young novelist should ever dare to imitate the style of Dickens. If such a one wants a model for his language, let him take Thackeray."

Since Trollope had no need to be envious of Dickens's financial success, for he had achieved financial success himself, and Dickens was dead and no longer a rival when the words were written, we may take them as the unbiased judgment of a very capable literary craftsman.

ANTHONY TROLLOPE
(1815–1882)

ANTHONY TROLLOPE

From the canvas by Samuel Laurence now in the
National Portrait Gallery

ANTHONY TROLLOPE

(1815–1882)

THERE is a memorial to Anthony Trollope in almost every street of every town, city, and village in the country. It was he who, when an official of the Post Office, originated the pillar box; first at St. Heliers in Jersey, and then throughout England.

It has become fashionable for the highbrow to scoff at Trollope, because he worked by the clock, or rather by his watch laid before him on his writing desk. He has also been described as a bad-tempered, unpleasant man, who bawled and bullied his way through life.

It is true that he had a vigorous personality. The office boy at Chapman & Hall's, the publishers', said he splashed around like a Triton in a school of minnows, and swore like a sergeant-major. Certainly he swore. Also, at his first interview with Mr. Chapman, the eminent publisher seemed ill at ease, and held the poker in his hand as a precaution. But Trollope was essentially sound. He was, as they say in the workshops, no half-inch mechanic, but a thorough craftsman. To him a job meant a job to be done as thoroughly, though as expeditiously, as possible.

For much of his life he hunted three days a week, and he has summed up his personality in this passage concerning his methods in the hunting field:

"Essex was the chief scene of my sport . . . few have investigated more closely than I have done the depth, and breadth, and water-holding capacities of an Essex ditch. It will, I think, be accorded to me by Essex men generally that I have ridden hard. The cause of my delight in the amusement I have never been able to analyse to my own satisfaction. In the first place, even now, I know very little about hunting—though I know very much of the accessories of the field. I am too blind (Trollope was short-sighted) to see the hounds turning, and cannot tell therefore whether the fox has gone this way or that. Indeed all the notice I take of hounds is not to ride over them.

"My eyes are so constituted that I can never see the nature of a fence. I either follow someone, or ride at it with the full conviction that I may be going into a horsepond or a gravel-pit. I have jumped into both one and the other.

"I am very heavy, and have never ridden expensive horses. I am also now old for such work (he was in the sixties) being so stiff that I cannot get on to my horse without the aid of a block or a bank. But I still ride after the same fashion, with a boy's energy, determined to get ahead if it may possibly be done, hating the roads, despising young men who ride them, and with a feeling that life can not, with all her riches, have given me anything better than when I have gone through a long run to the finish, keeping a place, not of glory, but of credit, among my juniors."

In short, nothing was going to stop Trollope from hunting or from writing novels.

His swearing, his bluster, his hard riding, and his almost infernal diligence as a novelist, can be explained on psychological grounds. In early life he was the dirtiest, scruffiest boy at Harrow, and afterwards the dirtiest, scruffiest boy at Winchester, and looked down on accordingly. The despised child grows up either a masochist or a thruster; either wormlike or unduly domineering and acquisitive. Trollope falls into the second category.

He came of most peculiar parents, both of them remarkable in different ways. He was the fourth son and fifth child of Frances and Thomas Anthony Trollope. His parents had seven children, some of whom died of consumption, except Emily the first, who died on the day on which she was born. They were Thomas Adolphus, Henry, Arthur William, Emily the first, Anthony, Emily the second, and Cecelia. Of these, Thomas Adolphus lived to be eighty-two, Henry died at the age of twenty-three, Arthur at the age of twelve, Emily the first aged one day, Emily the second at the age of eighteen. Cecelia married, but died of the family complaint aged thirty-three, having produced four children in the interval between birth and death. Anthony reached the age of sixty-seven.

Frances Trollope, Anthony's mother, was born in 1780 Frances Milton, younger daughter of the vicar of Heckfield and Mattingley, in north Hampshire. Attractive and witty, she fell just short of being beautiful, but in spite of her lively intelligence and charm people thought she would remain a spinster, since she put off marriage until what her period considered the incredible age of twenty-nine. In the year 1809 she married Thomas Anthony Trollope, a barrister, a fellow of New College, Oxford.

Her younger, and only, brother Henry introduced Thomas Anthony to her in 1808. This rather serious product of Winchester and New College was then thirty-four, and certainly an eligible bachelor, for he came of a good family, his grandfather, Sir Thomas Trollope, having been the fourth baronet. His mother's family enjoyed considerable wealth, and from it he anticipated a legacy. He was tall, with a commanding presence. It is true that he proposed to her in a rather pompous letter, an unromantic proceeding.

Frances, an honest girl, wrote back that all she owned in the way of fortune was £1,300, and a dress allowance of £50 a year from her father. This commendable accuracy in money matters she handed on to her son Anthony. She and Thomas Anthony were married, and began life in Bloomsbury, near her brother Henry, a clerk at the War Office. It was at his home, No. 27 Keppel Street—she and her husband lived at No. 16—that she had first met her husband.

Unfortunately, her husband's career at the Bar became less and less successful, owing to his unattractive temperament. He was sarcastic and cantankerous and over-bearing, and a barrister, like a doctor, needs a pleasing personality in order to succeed. Also he suffered from devastating headaches, which did not improve matters.

When his elder sons became old enough to go to school their father moved to Harrow, because at Harrow school children of local residents could enjoy free education. Rashly, in view of his declining practice, he leased a large estate and built a house on the leased estate. It was called "Julians" after the estate he hoped to inherit from his uncle, with whom, typically enough, he had quarrelled.

Trollope, who obligingly left us his autobiography, with

instructions that it should not be published until after his death, tells us that his father leased the land from Lord Northwick "in an evil hour", and that the farm was the grave of all his father's hopes, ambition and prosperity, the cause of his mother's sufferings and those of her children. It is to be doubted if Mrs. Trollope ever suffered a great deal. She took life, and even her gloomy husband, lightly; there seems always to have been someone from whom she could borrow money at a pinch, she had the same fiendish energy as her son Anthony, she made friends in the highest circles wherever she went; and anyway, there is no keeping down a woman who could, as she did, start a successful career as an authoress when turned fifty and the mother of seven children.

The father, Thomas Anthony, determined to use Harrow, where he had friends among the masters, as a preparatory school for Winchester for his sons, and three of them went to Harrow at the age of seven.

Trollope said that his boyhood was "as unhappy as that of a young gentleman could well be," attributing his unhappiness to a mixture of poverty and gentle standing on the part of his father, and a want on his own part of "that juvenile manhood" which lets some boys hold up their heads in adversity. It was at Harrow that Trollope developed his inferiority complex. By the time he reached the age of seven his father had let the big house, "Julians", and his house in London, and "descended", as Trollope puts it, to a farmhouse. His two brothers had been sent to Harrow as dayboarders from "Julians", and were probably received by "the aristocratic crowd" not as equals but as well as dayboarders were ever received. Trollope found himself "subjected to ignominy".

Dr. Butler, the headmaster, stopped him in the street, and asked him thunderously whether it was possible that Harrow School was disgraced by such a dirty little boy as he. Trollope adds dryly:

"He must have known me had he seen me as he was wont to see me, for he was in the habit of flogging me constantly. Perhaps he did not recognise me by my face."

After three years at Harrow Trollope was sent to a private school at Sunbury. There he found himself with no pocket money and few clothes. He found himself also one of four boys accused of "some nameless horror", innocent but believed to have been the guiltiest because, having come from a public school, he might be considered the black sheep of the accused. At the beginning of the next term the headmaster admitted that he might have been wrong. Trollope said nothing, but confessed in his autobiography:

"All that was fifty years ago, and it burns me now as though it was yesterday." The inferiority complex created at Harrow grew at Sunbury.

At twelve he continued to Winchester. It was the father's ambition that his three sons who were at Winchester should, as he had done, become fellows of New College. None of them did. The eldest brother, Thomas Adolphus, won three exhibitions from Winchester to Oxford, but missed the fellowship. The next two brothers died young. Trollope never went on to the University.

It was during his years at Winchester that the crisis in his father's affairs took place. Mr. Trollope relinquished his practice at the Bar, and retreated to a second farm. He nourished the illusion that anyone could be a farmer.

Mrs. Trollope then stepped into the breach, or attempted to do so. She conceived the fantastic idea of travelling to the United States and starting a bazaar in Cincinnati. She would take Henry with her and settle him there. She suggested that her husband should join them in a year's time. She sailed for New Orleans on November 4th, 1827, with her friend, Frances Wright, an ardent feminist who had evolved the project of founding a colony for the emancipation of slaves. Henry, his two sisters, Auguste Hervieu, an artist engaged as drawing master to the Nashoba colony (though why emancipated slaves should need a drawing master is not clear), and a manservant. M. Hervieu became worth his weight in gold. But for him Mrs. Trollope and her children might have starved.

Meanwhile, Trollope was faring no better at Winchester than he had fared at Harrow. It was then the Winchester custom to have the younger boys taught by the elder, and his brother, Thomas Adolphus, became Trollope's tutor. Part of Thomas's discipline took the form of thrashing his younger brother daily with a big stick. In time Thomas left Winchester to travel with his father to the United States, and there meet the adventurous Mrs. Trollope. The thrashings ceased, but still Trollope was not happy.

His father had left without paying his college bills, and the school tradesmen were told to refuse him credit. He could buy no clothes, and his companions, knowing his fees were unpaid, cast him out. He confesses:

"I suffered horribly. I could make no stand against it. I had no friend to whom I could pour out my sorrows. I was big, and awkward, and ugly, and I have no doubt skulked about in a most unattractive manner. Of course I was ill-dressed and dirty."

Worst of all, the second master, whose office it was to issue a shilling-a-week pocket money to boys, refused, in time, to give Trollope his shilling because his bills were unpaid. The other boys knew of the stoppage, and the reason for it. Periodically the boys gave their shillings to the college servants. The servant whose turn it was to receive this money found it a shilling short, and was told why.

"I never saw one of those servants," wrote Trollope, "without feeling that I had picked his pocket."

After three years at Winchester he was taken away by his father, who had left Mrs. Trollope, Henry, and the girls, in the United States, and the two of them lived "at a wretched tumble-down farmhouse on the second farm he had hired."

He returned to Harrow school as a day-boarder, walking the three miles from the farmhouse to school. He considered the eighteen months spent walking to and fro along the "miserably dirty lanes" the worst period of his life. All the boys at school despised him. He was turned fifteen, at a sensitive age for a boy, and longed for companionship on an equality with his schoolfellows. He learned nothing and the three hundred other boys ganged up against him. At last he rebelled, and "there came a great fight—at the end of which my opponent had to be taken home for a while".

Tom, his eldest brother, was at Oxford. Trollope and his father lived on the produce of the farm. Mr. Trollope was in debt to his landlord and his tradesmen. He occupied himself with writing a work which he called *Encylopaedia Ecclesiastica*.

It was to describe all ecclesiastical terms, including the denomination of every fraternity of monks and every convent of nuns, with all their orders and sub-divisions. It was not the type of book for which there could ever be a great demand; he was still working on it when he died, and only three numbers out of eight had been published by subscription.

We must now turn for a moment to Mrs. Trollope and her truly remarkable adventures in the United States.

Her voyage thither took seven weeks; the ship's bread was hard and the beef tough. She reached New Orleans on Christmas Day, went sight-seeing for a week, and then began the voyage up the Mississippi, leaving the river steamer at Memphis, whence Frances Wright galloped off on horseback in the direction of Nashoba. Mrs. Trollope had begun already to dislike Americans—she suffered from a serene admiration of all British institutions—and slavery seemed odd to her in a republic. However, the Trollopes followed Frances Wright on wheels, and the sight of Nashoba nearly finished them. The accommodation consisted of two-roomed cabins; the diet consisted of Indian meal and rain water. Mrs. Trollope perceived at once that she had been mistaken in Frances Wright, and made up her mind to leave; but to leave was impossible until she had borrowed three hundred dollars.

She decided, in spite of her experiences with Frances Wright, to send Henry to the communistic settlement founded by Mr. William Maclure, a rich Scottish philanthropist, on the Wabash river, known as New Harmony. The sixteen-year-old Henry could earn his living while being educated. She then departed with Auguste Hervieu, William the man-servant, and her two little girls to Cincinnati. She found the forefathers of the hamlet rude. Here Henry joined her in a state of chaos, having fled from New Harmony, where he had been made to work all day in the fields and bake his own bread at night. He had found the settlement more new than harmonious, and his health was shattered.

Sometime in the autumn Mr. Trollope arrived with Thomas Adolphus, having left Anthony languishing at Winchester. They had travelled steerage, and Mr. Trollope had suffered agonies, while Tom enjoyed himself. Mrs. Trollope rejoiced and gave a party to the provincials of Cincinnati. Mr.

Trollope and Tom left in February 1829 after the plans for the bazaar, which was to be Henry's, had been settled.

These plans were large, and the bazaar building combined in its architecture Saracen and Gothic influences. Before its completion Mrs. Trollope went down with malaria, and the plans fell to pieces. She became obliged to auction the unfinished building and sell the stock for the bazaar which her husband had sent from London. Mrs. Trollope, fifty years old, ill, and insolvent, did not lose heart. She determined to retrieve her fortune by writing a book on the United States, which Auguste Hervieu should illustrate.

In 1830 she sent Henry home to England, for fear that the summer climate of Cincinnati would kill him. She could not afford the fares for herself and the girls. She worked desperately at her book, managing at the same time to travel via Wheeling, West Virginia, to Maryland. No money arrived from England. She continued somehow to Philadelphia and New York, and New York pleased her. It seemed so civilised after Cincinnati and the West. On the whole, she liked most things about the United States except the inhabitants.

She arrived suddenly at the Harrow farm on August 5th, 1831. Her book, *The Domestic Manners of the Americans*, published on March 19th, 1832, won golden praises, including those of the dreaded *Quarterly Review*, and earned her £1,000. She began immediately a work of fiction entitled *The Refugee in America*. From then onward, until her death at the age of eighty-four, the amazing woman poured out a stream of novels and travel books numbering in all one hundred and fifteen volumes. Of these twelve were travel books and the rest novels. It cannot be doubted that Anthony Trollope inherited his industry in writing from his mother.

On the strength of her book, Mrs. Trollope moved her family back from the tumbledown farmhouse to the first farmhouse "which has since been called Orley Farm", from which Anthony had only a half-mile walk to school. His father wished him to go either to Oxford or Cambridge, in spite of money difficulties. But Anthony could not win an exhibition from Harrow; he tried for a sizarship at Clare Hall and a scholarship at Trinity, Oxford, and missed both, so that a university career became impossible.

He left Harrow shortly before his nineteenth birthday. He sums up his school life of twelve years in a grim mood. No attempt had been made to teach him anything but Latin and Greek, and he did little of either. He learned neither writing nor arithmetic, French nor German. Incredible as it sounds, when he applied for a clerkship in the Post Office he did not know the multiplication tables, and could not do a sum in long division. In spite of that, or because of it, he was a life-long opponent of the plan to recruit the Civil Service by means of examinations. He never won a prize at school. He believed he must have been in the writing master's class, but could not feel sure. He explains his doubt thus:

"I suppose I must have been in the writing master's class, but though I can call to mind the man, I cannot call to mind his ferule. It was by their ferules that I always knew them, and they me. I feel convinced in my mind that I have been flogged oftener than any human being alive. It was just possible to obtain five scourgings in one day at Winchester, and I have often boasted that I obtained them all. Looking back over half a century, I am not quite sure whether the boast is true; but if I did not, nobody ever did."

In March 1834 Trollope received instructions to drive his father, who was ill, up to London in the family gig. After they had started, Mr. Trollope explained that he was taking the Ostend boat, though he gave no reason for the voyage. When Trollope reached home, he found that the bailiffs were in. The gardener stopped him on the road, and pointed out that if he drove home the bailiffs would take the horse and gig as well, so Trollope drove into the village and sold horse and gig to the ironmonger for £17; the ironmonger then explained that £17 was exactly what Mr. Trollope owed him.

Trollope returned home, and found that his mother's personal belongings were being carried through a break in the hedge to their friend, Colonel Grant, who lived next door. His sisters and Colonel Grant's daughters performed this business. Mrs. Trollope and family stayed with the Grants for a few days and then followed Mr. Trollope to Belgium and settled down in a large house at Bruges; for Mrs. Trollope's ideas were always large, and lack of money made no difference to them.

The household numbered six: Mr. and Mrs. Trollope, Henry, Anthony, Emily, and Cecelia. The responsibility for keeping them fell on Mrs. Trollope, who was then fifty-five. She took it in her stride. Tragedy swooped down on her, for Mr. Trollope was ill and broken-hearted, though he still worked at his useless *Encyclopaedia Ecclesiastica*, while Henry and Emily had been diagnosed by a Bruges doctor as consumptives. Anthony, given the refusal of a commission in an Austrian cavalry regiment if he would learn French and German, became classics master in a school kept by a Mr. Drury, one of the Harrow masters during Anthony's first session there, at Brussels, so that he could study these languages. At the end of six weeks in Brussels he was offered a clerkship in the Post Office, and left for England. His mother had pulled strings through her best woman friend, Mrs. Clayton Freeling, whose father-in-law, Sir Francis Freeling, was Secretary to the Post Office.

Anthony returned to London by way of Bruges, and there saw the circumstances of that amazing parent. Mrs. Trollope, with the help of two Belgian maids, was nursing three dying patients, her husband, Henry, and Emily, on the one hand, and writing novels to support them on the other. She was capable of detaching her mind completely from her patients while she wrote, and from her writing table while she nursed. In order to have time for writing she rose at four a.m., and wrote until breakfast time. After that she nursed her sick. She had become rheumatic through suffering from malaria in the United States, and neuritis troubled her in her shoulders. Consequently, when her right arm was working, she slept one night with the help of laudanum, and wrote for three hours the next night, keeping herself awake on green tea.

Henry died on December 23rd, 1834, Mr. Trollope in February, 1835, and Emily in 1836.

Anthony's salary at the Post Office was to be £90 a year on which (he wrote):

"I was to live in London, keep up my character as a gentleman, and be happy. That I should have thought this possible at the age of nineteen, and should have been delighted at being able to make the attempt, does not surprise me now; but that others should have thought it possible, friends who knew something of the world, does astonish me."

Clayton Freeling, Anthony's sponsor, then Secretary at the Stamp Office, took him to St. Martin's le Grand, into the presence of the assistant secretary who, by some queer chance, was Henry Freeling, the Secretary's eldest son. This official asked Anthony to copy a passage from *The Times* with an old quill pen. He made several blots and spelling mistakes and Henry Freeling said:

"That won't do, you know." Clayton Freeling suggested that Anthony should do some writing at home and bring it next day. Henry Freeling enquired as to his arithmetic and Anthony, innocent of the multiplication table, replied:

"I know a little of it." Told that his examination in arithmetic would be held next day if his handwriting passed muster, he went home and made a fair copy of several pages of Gibbon. When he reached St. Martin's le Grand next day they gave him a desk and put him to work. No one looked at his fair copy, or examined him in arithmetic.

Trollope acknowledged that his first seven years in the Post Office "were neither creditable to myself, nor useful to the public service". He was supposed to arrive at his office punctually at ten a.m., and he seldom did. He was told that unless he reformed he would be dismissed. There was a clerks' sitting-room for the benefit of those on night duty, and after luncheon he would remain there playing *ecarté* for a couple of hours. There were also supper parties there at night, with card-playing, smoking, and the drinking of spirits. (Can one imagine these scenes of licence at the G.P.O. in these dull days?) In all this Trollope joined, on his £90 a year, and quite naturally ran into debt and ended in the hands of a money-lender.

Sir Francis Freeling died, and Colonel Maberley, who disapproved of Trollope, succeeded him. One day Trollope opened a private letter to the Colonel which was not marked private. It contained banknotes. He put it on the Colonel's table, where it was seen by him. The Colonel left the room and when he came back the letter had disappeared.

He sent for Trollope, and in the presence of a chief clerk, said to him:

"The letter has been taken, and, by God! there has been nobody in the room but you and I," and crashed his fist on the table.

"Then," said Trollope, "by God! you have taken it," and crashed his own fist down, not on the table but on a standing movable desk beside it on which stood a large bottle of ink. The ink splashed the Colonel's face and shirt-front; the chief clerk mopped him with blotting paper. The Colonel's private secretary entered the room with the letter and the banknotes. No more was said, but matters had not improved between Trollope and the Colonel.

A young woman in the country wished to marry him. "The invitation," he tells us, "came from her, and I had lacked the pluck to give it a decided negative". One day her mother arrived at the Post Office and entered the room where he sat with other clerks, a large basket on her arm, and an immense bonnet on her head. The messenger had been unable to keep her in the waiting-room. She said in a loud voice:

"Anthony Trollope, when are you going to marry my daughter?" This did not raise his superiors' opinion of his character, but he lived the matter down. There remained the moneylender. For the settling of a tailor's bill of £12 and £4 in cash, Trollope eventually paid him more than £200.

When he left the General Post Office after seven years' service his salary was only £140. By then he had reached the age of twenty-six. Often he could not afford the price of his dinner and he was always in debt. He found his only relaxation in an association with two other men, which they called the Tramp Society, its object being long walks in the counties round London. The one bright spot was that John (later Sir John) Tilley, a senior official in the Post Office, married Trollope's sister Cecelia, and became his good friend. But little went right for Trollope until, after seven years' service, a call came for volunteers to a new grade called surveyors' clerks.

There existed seven surveyors in England, two in Scotland, and three in Ireland. Pay and work for these new clerks were attractive. A clerk in the far west of Ireland proved unsuitable, and Trollope sought the hostile Colonel Maberley and asked for the appointment. The Colonel gave it him to get rid of him, sending to Ireland at the same time a very bad report on him. This change proved the turning point in Trollope's career.

It was August 1841. The Irish salary amounted only to £100 a year, but there were allowances of fifteen shillings a day for every day he was away from home, and sixpence for every mile travelled. One way and another the income totalled £400 a year.

The Trollopes always seemed able to borrow money in emergencies. Trollope approached the family lawyer, who was a cousin, and borrowed £200 to clear up his liabilities in England, collected a few letters of introduction from a fellow clerk at St. Martins le Grand, and reached Dublin on September 15th, 1841. Within a year he had become a valued servant of the Post Office.

Now, for the first time, we catch a light-hearted note in Trollope's confessions.

"It was altogether a very jolly life that I led in Ireland," he says, perhaps because in Ireland hunting had come into his life. The surveyor for whom he clerked kept a pack of hounds, though he never rode to hounds. It seems a peculiar state of affairs. Trollope therefore bought a hunter, and celebrated his record of the purchase with this lyrical passage on hunting:

"Then and thus began one of the great joys of my life. I have ever since been constant to the sport, having learned to love it with an affection which I cannot myself fathom or understand. Surely no man has laboured at it as I have done, or hunted under such drawbacks as to distances, money, and natural disadvantages. I am very heavy (towards the end of his life he weighed sixteen stone), very blind, have been—in reference to hunting—a poor man, and am now an old man. I have often had to travel all night outside a mail coach, in order that I might hunt the next day. Nor have I ever been in truth a good horseman. And I have passed the greater part of my hunting life under the discipline of the Civil Service.

"But it has been for more than thirty years a duty to me to ride to hounds; and I have performed that duty with a persistent energy. Nothing has ever been allowed to stand in the way of hunting—neither the writing of books, nor the work of the Post Office, nor other pleasures. As regards the Post Office, it soon seemed to be understood that I was to hunt; and when my services were re-transferred to England, no word of difficulty ever reached me about it. I have written on very many subjects, and on most of them with pleasure; but on no subject with such delight as that of hunting. I have dragged it into many novels—into too many no doubt—but I have always felt myself deprived of a legitimate joy when the nature of the tale has not allowed me a hunting chapter."

In Ireland he moved about, met people, investigated complaints, and in general found his feet as a human being. More important still, he gave satisfaction to his superiors, and enjoyed esteem for the first time in his life. It was in Ireland that he first began to write.

Always in his lonely boyhood he had told himself long serial stories with himself as the hero, a species of day-dreaming common among lonely people. The time was now due to put them on paper. Before he began, he had met the girl he was to marry.

She was Rose Heseltine; he met her at Kingstown, near Dublin, and they became engaged when he had been a year in Ireland. The wedding took place on June 11th, 1844, and all the money he possessed in the world was his income from the Post Office. He called his wedding day the commencement of his better life, and the marriage remained happy to its end.

He was now twenty-nine. Always he had made up his mind to write novels, but so far only the first volume of the first book existed. (This was the period of the three-volume novel.) He had mastered his work for the Post Office, and become a trusted official, but, as he said in his Autobiography:

"The vigour necessary to prosecute two professions at the same time is not given to everyone," and no one who has not done it can estimate the self-discipline it needs. On the credit side he had dealt with publishers in his mother's interest, and knew the great gulf which stretches between writing a book and having it published, and between having it published and winning success.

It was the sight of the ruins of a country house which gave him the idea for his first novel, *The MacDermots of Ballycloran*.

He finished it in July 1845, a year after his marriage, and sent the manuscript to his mother, who had influence among publishers. She agreed that she had better not read it before handing it to a publisher. None of the family believed he could write. He was not "the clever one of the family", that position being held by his elder brother, Thomas Adolphus.

A Mr. Newby, of Mortimer Street, undertook to publish *The MacDermots* and to divide the profits equally with the author. Trollope expected to receive nothing, and got nothing. The novel was a failure. Quite undaunted, he began *The Kellys and the O'Kellys*. Colburn published it in 1848, a year after the appearance of *The MacDermots*. The agreement was the same as that with Mr. Newby, and the result the same. And yet Trollope declared that he thoroughly enjoyed writing these books, and never expected anyone to read them.

Colburn's account showed that he had printed three hundred and seventy-five copies, sold one hundred and forty, and lost £62 10s. 1½d. He wrote to Trollope:

"It is evident that readers do not like novels on Irish subjects as well as on others. Thus you will perceive it is impossible for me to give any encouragement to you to proceed in novel-writing.

"As, however, I understand you have nearly finished the novel *La Vendée*, perhaps you will favour me with a sight of it when convenient."

In 1850, Colburn agreed to make an advance of £20 on *La Vendée*, pay a further £30 when he had sold three hundred and fifty copies, and £50 more if he sold four hundred and fifty copies within six months. This would be considered nowadays quite generous terms for the author of two unsuccessful novels.

La Vendée shared the fate of its two forerunners so far as the public was concerned, though its author had received £20. Not for years was he to make any more money by writing.

For a change Trollope decided to write a play, a fatal decision for the amateur who knows nothing of stage technique. He finished in 1850 a comedy partly in blank verse and partly in prose called *The Noble Jilt*, and sent it to an old actor friend, George Bartley, who was also an experienced stage-manager. Bartley took a grave view of *The Noble Jilt*. He had begun to read it, he wrote, with hopes, though it did not open dramatically. As he continued, his mood became gloomier. He ended:

"As to the character of your heroine, I felt at a loss how to describe it, but you have done it for me in the last speech of Madame Brudo (the heroine's aunt):

" 'Margaret, my child, never play the jilt again; 'tis a most unbecoming character. Play it with what skill you will, it meets but little sympathy!' And this, be assured, would be its effect upon an audience."

Since this was definitive, Trollope abandoned the play, thriftily using the plot later for a novel called *Can You Forgive Her ?*

There followed an Irish travel book, submitted to John Murray, the eminent publisher, which came to nothing. For the next two years Trollope was occupied completely with the Post Office, re-routeing rural deliveries, first in Ireland and then in England. He did the work on horseback, riding on an average forty miles a day. He explained:

"I was paid sixpence a mile for the distance travelled, and it was necessary that I should at any rate travel enough to pay for my equipage. This I did, and got my hunting out of it also."

The work proved fruitful to literature nevertheless. In the course of his journeys he reached Salisbury, and wandering about the neighbourhood of the Cathedral one summer evening he conceived the story of *The Warden*. From this idea grew the series now known as the Barchester chronicles, full of bishops, deans, and archdeacons.

"I may as well declare at once," said Trollope, "that no one at their commencement could have had less reason than myself to presume himself to be able to write about clergymen." He had never lived in any Cathedral city except London. His archdeacon ("for whom I confess I have all a parent's fond affection") was such as, in his opinion, an archdeacon should be, and he has been "declared by competent authorities to be an archdeacon down to the very ground". So in future no author need be deterred from writing about a type of which he knows nothing at all. He can always quote Trollope's archdeacon in extenuation.

On May 29th, 1853, he began *The Warden*, a year after conceiving the idea at Salisbury. He had only written the first chapter when he was appointed a surveyor in the Post Office, responsible for the northern counties of Ireland. He and his wife, and the two sons born to them, settled first at Belfast, and eighteen months later at Donnybrook, a suburb of Dublin. He was unable to continue *The Warden* until the end of 1853, and it was not completed until the end of 1854. The book appeared early in 1855. Messrs. Longman published it on a half profits basis. At the end of 1855 they paid him £9 8s. 8d. (Trollope is always accurate to the nearest penny), and at the end of 1856 a further £10 15s. 1d. As he said, "as regarded remuneration for the time, stone-breaking would have done better". Longmans printed one thousand copies, and after five or six years three hundred of these were converted into a cheap edition. No second edition was called for.

But the *Athenaeum* described the novel as "extremely clever and amusing", and it marked a turning point in Trollope's writing life. He had found his *milieu*, or, as he put it, "I was enabled to see wherein lay whatever strength I did possess . . . I had realised to myself a series of portraits, and had been able so to put them on the canvas that my readers should see that which I meant them to see. There is no gift which an author can have more useful to him than this."

Up to the end of 1857 he had received £55 for "the hard work of ten years;" literary work that is.

Following *The Warden* came *Barchester Towers*. For this Longmans offered him the half profits system with an advance of £100. They wanted him to cut the novel to two volumes instead of three, and he refused. It had about the same success as *The Warden*. In the long run, in the accumulation of what Trollope called further moderate payments, *The Warden* and *Barchester Towers* brought him £727 11s. 3d. for the two.

His next novel, *The Three Clerks*, produced a quarrel between him and Longmans. He wanted a lump sum down for it, Mr. Longman suggested that the name of Longman on the title page was worth more than an increased payment, and Trollope replied that he liked Longman's name best at the bottom of a cheque.

Getting no satisfaction, he took the novel to Hurst & Blackett, but as no one kept his appointment with the firm, he continued to the firm of Bentley, and sold the novel for £250.

In 1858 the Post Office asked him to go to Egypt and make a treaty for the conveyance of mails through Egypt by rail. At that time he was writing *Dr. Thorne.* Before departing for Egypt he asked Bentley for £400 for the copyright, and Bentley agreed, but announced the next day that, after further calculation, he could not offer more than £300. In a fury Trollope went to Chapman & Hall—it was that occasion on which Mr. Chapman held on to the poker—and sold his novel for £400.

Trollope crossed to France and continued to Marseilles, and from there had a rough voyage to Alexandria. He divided his time between writing and being seasick. It was now that he designed his method of writing, which he followed to the end of his literary career.

When he began a new book he made a diary divided into weeks and kept to it for the period which he allowed for the completion of the book. In this diary he recorded day by day the number of pages written, and if he failed to complete his tale of pages on one day he forced himself to make it up the next. He allotted himself about forty pages a week. Sometimes it fell to twenty and sometimes it rose to one hundred and twelve. A page contained two hundred and fifty words— four pages to the thousand words. The length of a novel is reckoned by the thousand words. Trollope commented on this system:

"A small daily task, if it be really daily, will beat the labours of a spasmodic Hercules. It is the tortoise which always catches the hare. The hare has no chance." All young persons who propose to write should take these words to heart. The man, or woman, with too little will-power to produce his daily tale of words should give up the idea of being a writer.

Trollope notes:

"While I was in Egypt, I finished *Dr. Thorne* and on the following day began *The Bertrams.*" That is a salutary statement. Directly the writer has finished one job he should begin another. It should have been noted in his work-sheet while he was still completing the previous task. No writer can afford to waste time.

"Had I," said Trollope, "taken three months of idleness between each they would have been no better," and this is perfectly true. "I . . . venture to advise young men who look forward to authorship as the business of their lives," he goes on, "to seat themselves at their desks day by day as though they were lawyer's clerks;—and so let them sit until the allotted task should be accomplished."

It is the only way in which to get books written.

He settled his postal treaty in two months when at last he reached Egypt, finishing *Dr. Thorne* in the intervals of diplomacy. The dilatoriness of negotiations afflicted his methodical mind, but he found satisfaction in getting his own way at last. He had intended that the mails should be carried through Egypt in twenty-four hours, and so they were. He returned home by way of the Holy Land, and inspected the Post Offices of Malta and Gibraltar. On his return Chapman & Hall paid him £400 for *Dr. Thorne* and promised a like amount for *The Bertrams*. It had been a fruitful and satisfactory journey.

Dr. Thorne became the most popular of his novels, judging from the sales, and nobody found a good word for *The Bertrams*. Trollope remained unmoved by the success of the one and the failure of the other. He had discovered that if he wrote a novel he could sell it, and if he wrote three in two years he could add £600 a year to his salary from the Post Office. He could keep a good house, insure his life, educate his two sons, and hunt twice a week on £1,400 a year. He did not dream idle dreams about literary fame. As is the case with all sensible writers, it was the money he wanted. You cannot pay school bills or rent with fame; if fame arrives as well as money it does no harm, but money there must be.

The reader will note the insistence on money by all the novelists whose biographies appear in this book, and they were perfectly right. The public must not expect masterpieces for nothing. The greengrocer and the butcher demand their reasonable profit, and so does the writer demand his, particularly as his job is far more exhausting than the greengrocer's or the butcher's.

But Trollope had now arrived in the Civil Service, as well

as in literature. When he returned from Egypt he received instructions to overhaul the Glasgow Post Office. In the autumn of that year (1858) he was asked to go to the West Indies and reorganise the Post Office there. His heart must have sunk, for in the autumn the hunting season begins, but he hurried at once to Chapman & Hall "demanding £250 for a single volume. The contract was made without difficulty and when I returned home the novel was complete in my desk".

The journey proved arduous, from Jamaica to Cuba, from Cuba to St. Thomas, and thence to Santa Martha, Carthagena, Aspinwall, over the Isthmus to Panama, up the Pacific to Costa Rica, across Central America, through Costa Rica, down the Nicaragua River to the Mosquito Coast, and home by Bermuda and New York. Throughout this long, long trail he wrote his weekly portion.

The book recorded his travels, and he made not a single note. It all came hot from the pen on the spot, and he considered the result the best of all his books. Reviews in *The Times* made his book's fortune, and he notes triumphantly:

"The result was immediate to me, for I at once went to Chapman & Hall and demanded £600 for my next novel," an increase, it will be observed, of £200 on what they paid for *Dr. Thorne* and *The Bertrams*.

After the West Indies journey the Post Office transferred him from Ireland to England. At first he feared that he would have to give up hunting, but "I thought that a man who could write books ought not to live in Ireland,—ought to live within reach of the publishers, the clubs, and the dinner parties of the metropolis." So he applied for a transfer, and became appointed to the Eastern District of England, which included Essex, Suffolk, Norfolk, Cambridgeshire, Hunts, and most of Herts.

It fell out that he was to continue his hunting for another sixteen years, mostly in Essex.

He proposed to move to England at the end of 1859. He was engaged on his novel *Castle Richmond*, but he had another project in view. The *Cornhill Magazine* was to be produced by Smith & Elder, under Thackeray's editorship, on January 1st, 1860. Trollope wished certain short stories of his to appear in that magazine, and wrote to Thackeray, whom at the time he did not know, on the subject. Thackeray replied in a

pleasant letter and Smith & Elder offered £1,000 for the copyright of a new novel to appear in *Cornhill*, on condition that
some of it should be delivered by December 12th (1859). The
offer came at the end of the October of that year.

This offer from Smith & Elder startled the methodical
Trollope. To think that *Cornhill*, to appear in January, still
lacked a serial in October! "I fear," he wrote gravely, "that
the answer to this question must be found in the habits of
procrastination which had at that time grown upon the
editor." Moreover, it was a fixed principle with him that no
part of a novel should appear until the novel was completed.
But Smith & Elder had offered £1,000, nearly double his last
offer from Chapman & Hall.

"If I now," wrote Trollope, "complied with the proposition
made to me, I must act against my own principle. But such a
principle becomes a tyrant if it cannot be superseded on a just
occasion." He concluded that the offer of £1,000 constituted
a just occasion.

Castle Richmond was half finished, but promised to Chap-
man & Hall. Trollope asked Edward Chapman if he could
cancel the contract if the story suited Smith & Elder. Mr.
Chapman said he could. But, continued Trollope, if *Castle
Richmond* did not suit Smith & Elder, could the Chapman &
Hall contract stand? The delightful Mr. Chapman said that
was as Mr. Trollope pleased. However, George Smith declined
Castle Richmond on the ground that it was an Irish story, and
Trollope produced *Framley Parsonage* for him instead. Trollope
describes the mixture of *Framley Parsonage* inimitably.

"There was a little fox-hunting and a little tuft-hunting,
some Christian virtue and some Christian cant. There was
no heroism and no villainy. There was much Church, but
more love-making. . . . Consequently they in England who
were living, or had lived, the same sort of life, liked *Framley
Parsonage*." It could hardly have failed of success since in it
appeared our old friends Mrs. Proudie and the archdeacon,
and Framley Parsonage stood near Barchester.

The *Cornhill* connection wafted Trollope into the literary
world of London which so far, on account of his Irish residence,
he had not entered. He took a house in Hertfordshire, part
of his new English postal district, twelve miles from London,

called Waltham House, and spent £1,000 on improvements. In January 1860 George Smith gave "a sumptuous dinner" to his contributors, and at this feast Trollope met Thackeray, G. H. Lewes, John (later Sir John) Everett Millais, who was illustrating *Framley Parsonage*, and other eminences.

"Sir Charles Taylor carried me home in his brougham. . . . He was our King at the Garrick Club, to which I did not yet belong."

A memorable evening.

When he had half-finished *Framley Parsonage* he turned from it to finish *Castle Richmond*, this being the only occasion on which he worked on two novels at the same time. *Castle Richmond* was not a success, perhaps because English readers, as Thackeray also discovered, simply will not read Irish stories for some reason. But what did Trollope care? He was entertaining friends at Waltham House, growing his own cabbages and strawberries, making his own butter, and killing his own pigs; by proxy of course. In 1861 the Garrick Club elected him, and when, two years later, Thackeray died, Trollope replaced him on the Committee. He took to club life like a duck to water:

"Having up to that time lived very little among men, having known hitherto nothing of clubs, having even as a boy been banished from social gatherings, I enjoyed infinitely at first the gaiety of the Garrick. It was a festival to me to dine there—which I did indeed but seldom, and a great delight to play a rubber in the little room upstairs of an afternoon." He is talking of the old premises in King Street; the Garrick Club now stands in Garrick Street.

The ostracism encountered in boyhood and early manhood had left him with a craving for acceptance by society. As he confessed:

"I have long been aware of a certain weakness in my own character, which I may call a craving for love. I have ever had a wish to be liked by those around me,—a wish that during the first half of my life was never gratified. In my school-days no small part of my misery came from the envy with which I regarded the popularity of popular boys. They seemed to me to live in a social paradise, while the desolation of my pandemonium was complete."

It was a very human weakness and a very human wish. He now entered his social paradise, becoming a member successively of the Arts Club, and of the Civil Service Club which he helped to found. In 1864 the Committee of the Athenaeum elected him, and in so doing set the seal on his success. If a man is elected to the Athenaeum, surely he has nothing left to pray for.

One day at the Athenaeum Trollope was sitting at the end of the long drawing-room writing *The Last Chronicle of Barset* when two clergymen sat down one on either side of the fire next him, each with a magazine in his hand. They began to complain about what they were reading, and each was reading a part of one of Trollope's novels.

"Here," said one clergyman, "is that archdeacon whom we have had in every novel he has ever written."

"And here," said the other, "is the old duke whom he has talked about till everyone is tired of him. If I could not invent new characters I would not write novels at all." The first clergyman then complained about Mrs. Proudie.

Trollope got up, introduced himself, and apologised.

"'As to Mrs. Proudie', I said, 'I will go home and kill her before the week is over'. And so I did." But he killed his old friend with many misgivings, he doubted if he could have done it except for the two clergymen, and sometimes, after he had killed her, he regretted the deed.

He wrote a second story for *Cornhill* in August 1861, called *The Struggles of Brown, Jones and Robinson*. He does not seem altogether to have mastered the knack of evolving happy titles. It was meant to be funny, and he thought it funny, but no one else did. The publisher "did not think it was equal to my usual work", the author confesses, adding briefly:

"I received £600 for it." It was not published in book form till 1870. Trollope said that his price had now become stabilised at £600 for "the quantity contained in an ordinary novel volume, or £3,000 for a long tale published in twenty parts, which is equal in length to five such volumes."

We have now followed Trollope from his struggles as a beginner at writing to the point of success. This is how he succeeded, told in his own words:

"The work I did during the twelve years that I remained

there (at Waltham House), from 1859 to 1871, was certainly very great. . . . Over and above my novels I wrote political articles, critical, social and sporting articles, for periodicals, without number. I did the work of a surveyor of the General Post Office, and so did it as to give the authorities of the department no slightest pretext for fault-finding. I hunted always at least twice a week. I was frequently in the whist-room at the Garrick. I lived much in society in London, and was made happy by the presence of many friends at Waltham Cross. Few men, I think, ever lived a fuller life. And I attribute the power of doing this altogether to the virtue of early hours.

"It was my practice to be at my table every morning at five-thirty a.m. An old groom, whose business it was to call me, and to whom I paid £5 a year extra for the duty, allowed himself no mercy. During all those years at Waltham Cross he was never once late with the coffee which it was his duty to bring me. . . . By beginning at that hour I could complete my literary work before I dressed for breakfast."

He considered that three hours a day "will produce as much as a man ought to write" but he must train himself to work continuously during those three hours. It had all this time been Trollope's custom "to write with my watch before me, and to require from myself two hundred and fifty words every quarter of an hour. I have found that the two hundred and fifty words have been forthcoming as regularly as my watch went."

This practice of writing by the watch has earned Trollope much contempt at the hands of "superior" writers and critics, but, oddly enough, their fame has not excelled his, or even equalled it. He writes of "all who have lived as literary men— working daily as literary labourers", and a literary labourer is what the professional writer is. Consequently, as Trollope points out, he should labour like other labourers, and that is the only way in which success will come to him. If he waits for the mood in which to work he will probably wait for ever, because no one likes work and the mood will never come. There is no such thing as what the amateur calls "inspiration". The writer who wants to succeed should sit at his writing table, in a not too comfortable chair, for regular hours every day, and train himself to write all the time he is sitting there. Writers, like babies, require to be trained in regular habits, and they must train themselves, since no one else can do it for them.

In spite of Mrs. Trollope's expedition to Cincinnati, and her wanderings about Europe, and long residence in Italy, Trollope became the most travelled member of the family. He had long wished to write a book about the United States ("My mother had thirty years previously written a very popular, but, as I had thought, a somewhat unjust book about our cousins over the water"). When the American Civil War broke out in 1861 he considered that a book on the United States would be topical, the obliging Chapman & Hall agreed to publish it, and, after a struggle, he obtained nine months' leave from the Post Office. He left England in August 1861 and returned in the following May, visiting all the States which had not seceded, except California.

"I worked," he said, "very hard at the task I had assigned to myself, and did, I think, see much of the manners and institutions of the people. Nothing struck me more than their persistence in the ordinary pursuits of life in spite of the war which was around them."

He commented on the completed book:

"My book . . . was not a good book. I can recommend no one to read it now in order that he may be either instructed or amused." There seems to be a doom hanging over English writers who write about the United States. Mrs. Trollope, her son, and Dickens all failed.

Before departing for the United States he had finished *Orley Farm*, which appeared in shilling numbers. His friends considered it his best novel, but he disagreed with them. By 1862 "I felt that I had gained my object . . . I had created for myself a position among literary men and had secured to myself an income on which I might live in ease and comfort. . . . From this time for a period twelve years my income averaged £4,500 a year. Of this I spent about two-thirds and put by one."

Oh, happy Trollope, at a time when income tax stood at a few pence in the pound, and surtax was non-existent.

It is impossible in this short sketch to catalogue and comment upon all Trollope's works, of which he lists forty-five at the end of his autobiography. Of his novels, his favourite was *The Last Chronicle of Barset* in which Mrs. Proudie was done to death at the instigation of a clerical member of the Athenaeum. It appeared in sixpenny parts, for the shilling magazines had interfered with the publication of novels in shilling numbers. ("Mr. Smith and I determined to make the experiment with sixpenny parts. As he paid me £3,000 for the use of my MS., the loss, if any, did not fall on me.")

But, he "cannot speak with too great affection of *Can You Forgive Her?*" made over, as we know, from the still-born play, *The Noble Jilt*. He explains that "that which endears the book to me is the first presentation which I made in it of Plantagenet Palliser, with his wife, Lady Glencora". Mr. Palliser appeared in *The Small House at Allington*, and in the last pages of it he marries the grand heiress of the day. He is nephew and heir to the Duke of Omnium, who also appears in *Dr. Thorne* and *Framley Parsonage*. Trollope spares them a typically Victorian comment of the

> " *God bless the Squire and his relations,*
> *And keep us in our proper stations* ".

type. Here it is, in all its grandeur:
"In these personages and their friends, political and social, I have endeavoured to depict the faults and frailties and vices, —as also the virtues, the graces, and the strength of our highest classes; and if I have not made the strength and virtues predominant over the faults and vices, I have not painted the picture I intended. Plantagenet Palliser I think to be a very noble gentleman,—such a one as justifies to the nation the seeming anomaly of an hereditary peerage and of primogeniture."

Those curious to become acquainted with this noble gentleman *ab ovo usque ad mala*, from the soup to the savoury, should read *Can You Forgive Her?*, *Phineas Finn*, *Phineas Redux*, and *The Prime Minister* in that order.

In 1865 Trollope and some associates founded the *Fortnightly Review*. They decided that it should represent freedom of speech combined with personal responsibility, but Trollope insisted that nothing should appear denying or questioning the divinity of Christ. They made G. H. Lewes (see the biography of " George Eliot ") editor, and as the distributing trade disliked a fortnightly publication, turned it into a monthly, at the same time retaining the title. When they had spent all their capital they sold the copyright to the ever-obliging Chapman & Hall.

Trollope was also one of the founder-members, as one might put it, of the *Pall Mall Gazette*, founded by the untiring George Smith, of Smith & Elder, in 1865. Smith flung into this enterprise the talents of all the literary men connected with his publishing business and *Cornhill*, of whom Trollope was not the least. But he did not care for newspaper work.

"I was fidgety when any word was altered in accordance with the judgment of the editor, who, of course, was responsible for what appeared. I wanted to select my own subjects,—not to have them selected for me; to write when I pleased,—and not when it suited others."

These things cannot be on a newspaper, and so:

"As a permanent member of the staff I was no use, and after two or three years I dropped the work."

In 1867, Mr. James Virtue, a printer and publisher, offered Trollope £1,000 a year to edit a magazine, with payment on space for his contributions. He took a gloomy view of the project, and advised Mr. Virtue to abandon it; Mr. Virtue replied that if Trollope did not edit the magazine, somebody else would.

He therefore assumed the editorship of a magazine ultimately called *St. Paul's*, and Mr. Virtue lavished money on the venture. A glittering necklace of contributors adorned it, and never was so little accomplished by so many. It seldom exceeded a circulation of 10,000, and died quite painlessly.

Trollope had resigned from the Post Office in the autumn of 1867, just before taking over the editorship of the ill-fated *St. Paul's*, relinquishing a pension in so doing. The chief reason seems to have been that he asked for the post of Under-Secretary, his brother-in-law being Secretary, but the appointment went to a Mr. Scudamore. The Secretary, in accepting the resignation, wrote a flattering letter which Trollope

describes as "official flummery", in which occurred the glow-
ing phrases:

"You have for many years ranked among the most conspicuous members of the Post Office, which, on several occasions when you have been employed on large and difficult
matters, has reaped much benefit from the great abilities
which you have been able to place at its disposal." And these
words were not ill-chosen. He had done well by the Post
Office; and hunted, and written novels into the bargain.

One of his sons had felt the Call of the Wild when the time
arrived to make a career, and departed to the great wide-open
spaces of Australia to become a sheep farmer, if that is the
correct expression. Trollope referred to him as his shepherd
son. In the spring of 1871, his parents agreed to visit him.
("Of course before doing so I made a contract with a publisher for a book about the Colonies.") They decided to leave
Waltham Cross, and live in London on their return, and sold
most of their furniture.

They sailed from Liverpool in May 1871, leaving *Ralph the
Heir* running in *St. Paul's*. The editor of the *Fortnightly Review*
had *The Eustace Diamonds* ready to begin publication in the
following July. Left behind in a strong-box were *Phineas Redux*,
sold later to the Graphic, and *An Eye for an Eye*, unpublished
when the autobiography was written. On board ship Trollope
had a desk in his cabin, and before they reached Melbourne
he had finished *Lady Anna* (sold later for £1,200). It was
written "during the two months required for our voyage, and
was done day by day—with the intermission of one day's
illness—for eight weeks, at the rate of sixty-six pages of manuscript in each week. . . . Every word was counted. I have
seen work come back to an author from the press with terrible
deficiencies as to the amount supplied."

There was no stopping the man; but the Trollopes would
not starve.

They stayed five happy weeks with the young shepherd and
his sheep ("he was not making money, nor has he made
money since. . . . But I rejoice to say that this has been in no
way due to any fault of his") and then Trollope, wishing to
write a book about what he called the entire group of Aus-
tralasian Colonies, settled at Melbourne, and from there

investigated Queensland, New South Wales, Tasmania, "the very little-known territory 'of Western Australia", and New Zealand. The whole journey took eighteen months; the book was written while travelling, and he reached England in December 1872 with the book almost finished. It brought in £1,300.

Joyfully he turned to hunting, first in Essex, and then at Leighton Buzzard with Baron Meyer and Mr. Selby Lowndes ("I did not care so much for Mr. Lowndes.") Four years later, in April 1876, we have the sad note:

"Now at last . . . I do think that my resolution is taken. I am giving away my old horses, and anyone is welcome to my saddles and horse-furniture", and the melancholy quotation:

> " I've lived about the covert side,
> I've ridden straight and ridden fast ;
> Now breeches, boots, and scarlet pride
> Are but mementoes of the past."

They took a house in Montagu Square and settled themselves. There were more novels, until we reach the passage in the autobiography:

"And so I end the record of my literary performances,—which I think are more in amount than the works of any other living English author." There follows a detailed statement of receipts from 1847 to 1879, which totals £68,939 17s. 5d. Like the other subjects of this biography, except Meredith, Trollope did not make old bones. In the early summer of 1880 his doctors sent him to the country on account of what they told him was asthma, though it was really heart disease. He took a house in Harting, West Sussex. It had five acres of ground, and if he could not run sheep, like his son, he could have an assortment of domestic animals.

He was still working: on lives of Cicero and Lord Palmerston, at novels entitled *Kept in the Dark*, and *The Fixed Period*. When *The Fixed Period* came to an end he visited Italy, where lived his elder brother, Thomas Adolphus. The visit lasted a fortnight, and on the way home, in March 1881, he began *Mr. Scarborough's Family*. In February 1882 he began *An Old Man's Love*.

H

There is something pathetic about Trollope at this stage, because the public has begun to forget him. *Kept in the Dark* and *The Fixed Period* brought only £450 each. Chapman & Hall cut the price of *Ayala's Angel* from £1,500 to £1,150. *All the Year Round* paid no more than £400 for the serial rights of *Mr. Scarborough's Family*.

Then there flared up the ancient spirit of Trollope. In the past when one publisher refused his price he had always gone to another. Accordingly he sought the new firm of Chatto & Windus, and in September 1882 made two novel contracts at £600 each.

He settled for the winter with his wife at Garland's Hotel, in Suffolk Street, Pall Mall. It was to be his last winter. On November 4th, after dinner, at the house of his brother-in-law, Sir John Tilley, he suffered a grave seizure. They took him to a nursing home in Welbeck Street, and after ten days he could walk, though he could not speak.

On December 3rd, Sir William Jenner, the famous consultant of the period, gave little hope of his recovery, and at six o'clock in the afternoon of December 6th he died. They buried him at Kensal Green, and among those present at the funeral were Browning, Millais, who had illustrated his novels, and Chapman, the faithful publisher.

When one searches for an adjective with which to describe Trollope, one falls back inevitably on the rather dreadful adjective "sound". He was essentially a sound man and a sound writer. He claimed to be no more, and his best epitaph may be found in his own words:

"I do lay claim to whatever merit should be accorded to me for persevering diligence in my profession. . . . I have never been a slave to this work, giving due time, if not more than due time, to the amusements I have loved. But I have been constant,—and constancy in labour will conquer all difficulties. *Gutta cavat lapidem non vi, sed saepe cadendo.*" (The drop hollows the stone not by strength, but by always falling.)

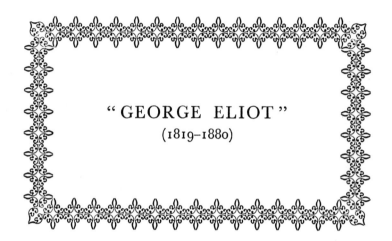

" GEORGE ELIOT "

(1819–1880)

"GEORGE ELIOT"

From a replica of the canvas by François D'Albert Durade
now in the National Portrait Gallery

"GEORGE ELIOT"
(1819–1880)

IT WILL be simpler in this biography to refer to the great woman novelist who signed her novels "George Eliot" as Mary Ann. She lived for twenty-four years with George Henry Lewes, from whom she borrowed the first half of her pen name, and two Georges tend to confusion. The second half of her pen name she chose because, as she said, "Eliot was a good mouth-filling easily pronounced name."

Mary Ann was essentially middle class, and in her novels she wrote about the middle class. She had an enormous capacity for taking pains and acquiring facts, most unusual in a woman. She was not beautiful, but she possessed one asset of beauty, her mass of red-brown hair. It is typical of her that she let a phrenologist shave it off in order the more conveniently to examine her "bumps". Nothing, not even her hair, must be allowed to obstruct the acquisition of knowledge.

Her dogged determination and her passion for facts she inherited from her father, Robert Evans, the son of George Evans, a builder and carpenter in the Derbyshire village of Norbury. Robert was born in 1773 and began life, after he had learned to read and write, as an apprentice in his father's business. There he did well, but when he came of age he threw up building and carpentering in favour of farming. He rented a small, poor farm, and became a notable farmer, so notable that in 1799 the owner of the farm offered him the post of agent over all his property.

Robert accepted the offer, and reorganised local methods of farming. In 1801 he married, and became in time the father of a boy Robert and a girl Frances. His employer, a Mr. Newdigate, inherited the Arbury estate, and Robert went with him to Warwickshire and found himself responsible for a forest, the forest of Arden, among other things. The forest appealed to him.

His wife died in 1809 but Robert went on and prospered, and prepared to marry again. His second wife was Christiana Pearson and the Pearsons owned property and were "gentry". Christiana became fascinated by Robert's enormous strength and knowledge of farming and forestry, but when Robert asked for her her father refused. The entire family rose up against him as a husband for Christiana, but she and he carried on a secret love affair until she came of age and said she would please herself about her husband. She and Robert were married on February 8th, 1813.

They lived in great happiness, and Robert became agent to Colonel Newdigate, the nephew of his employer Francis Newdigate, Lord Aylesford, Lord Lifford, and a Mr. Bromley Davenport all at once. In 1814 the first child of his second marriage was born, a girl called Christiana after her mother. Two years later his wife bore a son, Isaac. On November 22nd, 1819, she bore a second daughter, Mary Ann Evans, who was to become famous as "George Eliot" the novelist.

Mary Ann, his last child, fascinated her father, whom she resembled in many ways. In March 1820 a change most important for her took place in the family circumstances. Robert, her father's son by his first wife, had already become agent for the Kirk Hallam farm, on which Robert the elder had made his first experiment in farming, and Frances, his daughter by his first wife, had gone with her brother to keep house for him. Mr. Newdigate now offered Robert an old red brick house called Griff on the Arbury Estate, and he accepted it eagerly. Griff was a large, delightful old house, more important and spacious than the one he was occupying. More, it set the seal on his success in life, for it was the house of a "gentleman".

Griff was to be Mary Ann's home for twenty-one years, and many features of this charming, red-brick, ivy-covered house were reproduced when she described the childhood of Maggie and Tom Tulliver in *The Mill on the Floss*. Every corner of every field remained in her memory; there she formed, in her very early years, the close companionship with her brother Isaac which was to be broken later.

When she was turned four she was sent to a kindergarten school kept by a Mrs. Lathom at Attleboro, two miles from

Griff, where she found herself the youngest child in the school, and hated to be alone in her bedroom in the dark. Every week-end she returned home, and renewed her companionship with Isaac, who laughed at her because she was a girl, though she could read better than he. Disillusionment came on Isaac's tenth birthday. Mary Ann had saved up all her money to buy him a present, but he only thanked her casually and invited her to come into the yard and see his present from their father. Mary Ann followed him and Isaac mounted the pony which his father had given him and rode away.

Mary Ann decided to find her consolation in books, which she read so much more easily than did Isaac. She read *Aesop's Fables*, and *Joe Miller's Jest Book*, and settled finally to read *Waverley*. Before she had read more than half she found that *Waverley* had been returned to the friend who had lent it.

Thereupon the astounding child of eight sat down to finish *Waverley* herself from where she had left off reading. She wrote and wrote, and her astonished parents did not interfere. Robert Evans read what she had written, and was so impressed that he borrowed *Waverley* again, so that Mary Ann could compare her story with Sir Walter Scott's. She preferred her own to Sir Walter's, and continued to read, including in her discoveries Lamb's *Essays* and *The Pilgrim's Progress*; however, her favourite book was Defoe's *The History of the Devil*.

Robert Evans considered that all this reading indicated the need for a superlative education. He found a suitable school at Nuneaton, and one of the mistresses, a Miss Lewis, undertook to keep a special eye on Mary Ann. Miss Lewis and she became close friends; not only did the governess teach her the normal subjects, but she instructed her in religion. Miss Lewis was a Calvinistic Baptist. One way and another, Miss Lewis managed to retain Mary Ann's friendship long after she left Nuneaton.

Her stay there lasted only a short time and she continued to a school of great repute in Coventry, kept by the Misses Franklin, the daughters of a Baptist minister. For them and their father Mary Ann also conceived a great regard.

If Miss Lewis had been addicted to religion, the Misses Franklin were fanatical, and, aided by their father, they made a proselyte of Mary Ann. She led the other girls in prayer, and gave the eggs her father sent her to such girls as lacked these delicacies.

Then it came to pass that she attended a service of the Church of England and the music entranced her, though she had been taught that religious music was wrong. All her life she displayed a passion for music, and the music in the Coventry church set up in her religious doubts. But at Christmas 1835 her father became seriously ill and Mary Ann returned home. Her mother fell ill also, and though her father recovered, when summer had passed her mother was dead.

Mary Ann's return to school became delayed; she roamed about Griff heartbroken at her mother's death, her only comfort the religion she had learned at school, which was all about hell-fire, and that sort of thing. Then her sister Christiana married a doctor, and Mary Ann took over the care of her father's house. She was now seventeen.

Her father, on the other hand, was sixty-three. Shakespeare has pointed out that crabbed age and youth cannot live together, and although nowadays we do not consider a man of sixty-three to be in his old age, in the year 1836 a countryman of sixty-three was a good deal older, mentally at any rate, than his modern counterpart. Mary Ann sympathised with the contemporary aspirations of the young, and Robert Evans did not. He had no patience with Reform—he had done very well without Reform—but Mary Ann approved of it, or at any rate did not disapprove. Gradually Robert gave up one thing after another in disgust, and as he gave it up, so his daughter took it over.

She had already the entire care of the house; next she took over the garden, and six months later the dairy. Finally Robert abandoned his farm, and Mary Ann took that over too, earning the respect of the local farmers by her results.

"She boggled at nothing," declares one of her biographers, whatever boggling is. But there was also her religion which troubled her. The Misses Franklin (and their father) had taught her that pleasure was a sin, beauty was a sin, and every secret wish must be denied. Mary Ann had not much time for sins of pleasure and beauty, what with the garden, and the dairy, and the house, and the farm, and one thing and another, but she played for safety, and in her spare time preached in the village, gave away milk puddings, and sat up at night with the sick.

She even tried to convert her brother Isaac, who hunted, raced, played cards, and went to the theatre, but he only laughed at her. This hurt her very much. As a consolation she took lessons in German and Italian from a Mr. Brezzi, who had taught at the Misses Franklin's school. It is not known exactly how she fitted these lessons in with all the rest. Her Coventry music teacher, a Mr. M'Ewen, also called at Griff to continue his instruction.

After a time she began to hate Griff. She wanted leisure to read serious books, and we have seen how much leisure she could find at Griff. Isaac took her to London, but she refused to go out with him in the evening, and stayed behind reading Josephus's *History of the Jews* and Hannah More's *Letters*.

In the New Year (1837) her aunt, Mrs. Samuel Evans, came to stay at Griff. Mrs. Evans was a Methodist and had preached in the fields. Mary Ann confessed what she believed to be her sins to her aunt, who listened with patience, quoting appropriate texts, and felt better. By 1840 she discovered a longing to publish something and sent some verses to the *Christian Observer*, which were printed, with her initials at the end.

Her appetite whetted, she began something more ambitious: a *Chart of Ecclesiastical History*, containing the Roman Emperors, poetical and religious history of the Jews, the Bishops . . . the aspect of heathenism and towards Christianity, chronology of the Apostolical and Patristical writings, schisms, and heresies . . . "and I thought possibly an application of the Apocalyptic prophecies".

This, naturally, meant a certain amount of reading, and Mary Ann read. She imported vast quantities of books from London. Unfortunately someone else had conceived the same idea, and finished his book; news came that it would be published very soon. Mary Ann did not lament; at any rate she had learned a lot through her reading.

Now at last there came a change in her life. Her brother Isaac was to be married, and Robert Evans decided to let his son have Griff, and live in Coventry with Mary Ann. They took a house in Foleshill Road, then on the fringe of

Coventry; a large house with a garden. And in Coventry Mary had a harbinger, or rather two harbingers, none other than the Misses Franklin. No more distinguished pupil than Mary Ann had ever graced their educational establishment, and they spread the news of her virtues at large, while Mary Ann waited at home and no callers arrived. Unfortunately, the world being what it is, the Misses Franklin's description of her virtues had frightened everyone away.

However, her house was semi-detached, and a Mrs. Pears, sister of a Mr. Charles Bray who lived next door, took the risk, and found it well worth taking, because Mary Ann, apart from her astonishing mass of knowledge, was an unaffected, charming country girl. And she confessed to Mrs. Pears that the condition of the factory hands in Coventry distressed her. What did Mrs. Pears think she should do? Would giving them milk puddings be any good?

Mrs. Pears temporised by introducing her brother, Charles Bray, and Mary Ann met him on November 2nd, 1841. He was a rich ribbon manufacturer, a free-thinker, and the author of *The Education of the Feelings*, and *The Philosophy of Necessity*. There was also his wife, Caroline, a charming creature, sister of Charles Hennell, who was young and had written *An Inquiry Concerning the Origin of Christianity*.

Very naturally, Mary Ann tried to convert Charles Bray from his free-thinking. In return, since he studied and believed in phrenology, she allowed him to examine her head. Charles Bray lent her his books, which she read most carefully, and to her alarm found that, instead of her converting him, his books were converting her.

She realised that Christianity had failed by acquiescing in slums and poverty, and that Christ's personality and teaching had been smothered by all the fanfaronade of the Churches.

Mary Ann was a direct young woman. Having abandoned her religion, she wrote and acquainted the Misses Franklin with the fact. They sent a Baptist minister to reason with her, but, having a far better brain than his, she utterly defeated him.

The Misses Franklin being defeated, she then tackled her father. She explained to him that she would be unable to go to church again.

This was at night after supper. Robert Evans merely replied that she was talking stuff and nonsense, or in words to that effect, and told her to go to bed; and although now twenty-three years old she obeyed and went to bed. The cure did not work, and in the morning, with female persistence, she repeated what she had said overnight, with the consequence that neither spoke to the other for many days. At last Robert Evans put his foot down; if she refused to change her mind about going to church he would sell the house and live at Griff with Isaac and his wife. Mary Ann replied that he could for all she cared; she was perfectly able to earn her living as a governess.

Since Robert Evans had no wish to return to Griff, he wrote to Isaac about the unbelievable behaviour of Mary Ann, and though Isaac, as we know, went racing, and to the theatre, and played cards, the behaviour of his sister shocked him. She was sent back to Griff that Isaac might reason with her, and at first she refused to alter her mind. But even Mary Ann was human; Isaac and the Brays persuaded her that, just as Paris was worth a Mass, the delights of Coventry were worth attendance at morning service. Mary Ann agreed to attend in order to please her father, retaining her private convictions.

As a consolation she made two new friends in Sara, Mrs. Bray's sister, and Charles Hennell. Sara was a free-thinker, and Charles had written the *Inquiry concerning the Origin of Christianity*, a book which had impressed Mary Ann deeply. Consequently, when Charles, who was thirty, arrived in Coventry, she, aged twenty-three, fell in love with him. She had never been in love before, and it was time.

Charles was not only handsome, but also completely free from worry about hell-fire, Christian dogma, and all the rest of it. He seemed to her to live in a state of almost delirious mental freedom. She walked and talked with him all the summer of 1842, and wished that she were pretty; but her only beauty was her thick brown hair, and she could hardly be described as glamorous. After all, it is the glamorous qualities of a woman which appeal to a normal man, so that, unfortunately though Mary Ann fell in love with Charles, he did not fall in love with her.

Worse still, there arrived a Miss Brabant, daughter of a

German savant, not only clever but good-looking. She had decided to translate Strauss's *Life of Jesus*. Charles Bray and Charles Hennell fell at her feet, but as Charles Bray already had a wife it was Charles Hennell who married Miss Brabant, and Mary Ann could not be comforted. She consoled herself at length by translating Strauss's *Life of Jesus* since Miss Brabant-that-was now had more exciting occupations. She worked so hard at it that she became ill.

Mr. and Mrs. Bray took her in hand and carried her off to the Cumberland Lakes, where she rowed and climbed mountains. Mary Ann, who was young and strong, recovered from overwork and her love affair alike ànd returned to Coventry a new young woman, where Charles Bray proceeded to fall in love with her, or so it appeared, for he would never, if he could help it, let her out of his sight. At last he called on her and found her alone. After talking a long time to gather his courage, he asked the question he had been dying to ask her for weeks. It was not the question Mary Ann had anticipated. Charles did not beseech her to be his mistress. He begged her to shave her head and let him examine it. His interest in her was purely phrenological.

Mary Ann consented. She went to London with Charles and his wife, a party of phrenologists gathered, her head was shaved, and a plaster cast made of it. Charles confessed he had learned nothing and Mary Ann was obliged to wear a cap till her hair grew again.

Three years after she had begun it she finished the translation of Strauss's *Life of Jesus*. Her publisher gave her £20 for all rights in it. She felt horrified, but she accepted the small sum. There was nothing else to do. The book was published on June 15th, 1846.

Robert Evans now began to fail, and she longed for some distraction from the dull part of the devoted daughter. Her *Life of Jesus* had earned applause, and so she sat down to translate Spinoza's *Tractatus Theologico-Politicus* from Latin into English. It sounds a dreadful occupation for a young woman of twenty-five, but it probably saved Mary Ann from being driven mad by her senile parent. He was dying, but he would not die. However, the end came on May 31st, 1849.

Once more the Brays saved Mary Ann from physical collapse. They were leaving for a month's tour of the Continent, and they insisted on taking her with them. On June 11th the party set forth, to visit Paris, Lyons, Avignon, Marseilles, Geneva, Milan . . . and halted finally at Geneva. There the Brays left Mary Ann and returned home. Mary Ann remained alone. Let her brother Isaac settle her father's estate.

In Geneva she made friends, very different friends from those at Coventry: an Austrian baron and baroness, a French marquis and marquise, a German baron.

In October of that year (1849) she took lodgings in the town of Geneva at 150 francs a month, with an artist and his wife, a Monsieur and Madame d'Albert. She dined with them and breakfasted in her room, and made of them two firm friends. It was not to be a passing friendship, for in the years to come Monsieur d'Albert was to translate *Adam Bede*, *The Mill on the Floss*, *Silas Marner*, *Romola* and *Scenes from Clerical Life*.

Mary Ann hired a piano, and with that and the d'Alberts found herself perfectly happy.

In March 1850 she returned to England, escorted by Monsieur d'Albert, and arrived at Griff, where her brother Isaac and his wife lived. She did not find her welcome very cordial, and continued to her sister Christiana's house. Christiana had just lost a baby, such a common experience with early Victorian mothers. Unfortunately for Mary Ann, Christiana was not like

> " *A little child with heart so wide*
> *It takes the whole world in.*"

She had her husband and her home and her personal affairs and there seemed no room in her life for her sister as well. Outwardly she was so unbearably kind and considerate that Mary Ann, at screaming point, departed to Rosehill, Coventry, the home of Charles and Caroline Bray. There she was happy, even if Charles had once insisted on shaving off all her hair to learn precisely nothing.

In the cosy surroundings of Rosehill she began her journalistic life. The editor of the *Coventry Herald* asked her to review books, and she reviewed Mackay's *Progress of the Intellect*. She sent a copy of the *Coventry Herald* containing her article to the *Westminster Review*, and lo, in January 1851 that review also printed it. It found favour, and Mr. Chapman, of the *Review*, who was a friend of Charles Bray, came down to visit Charles and met Mary Ann.

She possessed an overwhelming personality, and she overwhelmed Mr. Chapman. Soon he found himself asking her to write a series of articles for the *Westminster Review*. She wrote them, and its readers were delighted, and Mr. Chapman made an excuse to visit Charles Bray again, and offered Mary Ann an appointment as assistant editor of the *Westminster Review*. He had found her a pearl from the point of view of this periodical, and wished her to be his pearl and his only.

Mary Ann leaped at the proposal, and in September 1851 repaired to London, where Mr. and Mrs. Chapman offered her rooms in their house, 142 Strand. Besides prattle about the Great Exhibition in Hyde Park, there are at this time two significant entries in her diary:

"I was introduced to Lewes the other day . . . a sort of Mirabeau in appearance."

"On Friday we had . . . a Mr. Herbert Spencer who has just brought out a large work on *Social Statics* which Lewes pronounces the best work he has seen on the subject."

All her life Mary Ann carried the art of being busy to a very high pitch, and at 142 Strand she scarcely found an idle moment between her social life and her work in the *Westminster Review*. Yet the time, and the man, arrived, to tempt her to indulge in a little idle dalliance under the apple trees in Mr. Chapman's garden, that garden which bordered the river.

So far there had only been Charles Hennell; now there was Herbert Spencer, a year younger than herself, good-looking, and attractive to women. They met first on a mental plane, but to Mary Ann Herbert Spencer soon meant far more than the author of a book on social statics; he aroused her emotions, whereas, so far as we can judge, Spencer wanted no more than intellectual flirtation. Mary Ann, for her part, confessed that without him her life would be desolate enough.

The attentions of Spencer continued, without definite result, for months and months, and she became pale and listless, reviving when Spencer's father arrived in London and called on her. But in time the father departed, and the son's visits grew less frequent, and Mary Ann could not make him out at all. She knew the truth when at last he dropped her altogether, dismissing her later in his autobiography in these words:

"There were reports that I was in love with her and that we were about to be married. But neither of these reports was true."

She decided to move from the Chapmans' house which, with the garden and the apple trees, reeked of Herbert Spencer, and look for lodgings. Yet, although she did not perceive the fact at once, the cloud created by Herbert Spencer had a silver lining; someone else was at that very moment entering her life, never to leave it until death took him from her. George Henry Lewes began quietly to make himself indispensable to her. It was he who found her lodgings in the end, at 21 Cambridge Street, Hyde Park.

Let us glance for a moment at G. H. Lewes, for he will shortly become Mary Ann's inseparable companion, and finally her lover.

He was born in London, the grandson of the comedian, Charles Lee Lewes, in 1817, being two years older than she. He had been educated in Jersey and Brittany as well as at Greenwich, and began his career in a lawyer's office, left that for commerce, tried medicine but could not face operations, and spent two years in Germany.

Returning to London in 1840 he made an effort to become an actor like his father, but gave it up and began contributing to penny encyclopaedias, the *Morning Chronicle*, and a number of reviews and magazines. From 1851, the year in which Mary Ann came to London, until 1854 he edited the *Leader*.

Nothing in his appearance made him attractive to women. He wore a Victorian cavalry sergeant-major's moustache, and a Newgate fringe, while his curly hair, thinning on top, stuck out at the sides like a bush. Frequently he wore his tie askew, but he had a good brow, and it was the things of the mind which first linked him with Mary Ann, herself no beauty apart from her thick brown hair.

Like hers, his life had not run smoothly. He had made a marriage in 1840 which turned out unhappily, and could not obtain a divorce. He developed into one of the famous dramatic critics, and few men have contrived a more versatile career. Frederick Harrison wrote of him that he "began life as a journalist, a critic, a novelist, a dramatist, a biographer, and an essayist; he closed it as a mathematician, a physicist, a chemist, a biologist, a psychologist, and the author of a system of abstract general philosophy."

Only his novels, *Ranthorpe* (1847) and *Rose, Blanche and Violet* (1848), lacked literary merit; he wrote one successful play, *The Game of Speculation*, and two that failed. His best-known work is his *Life and Works of Goethe* (2 vols., 1855) which became the standard English life, and sold sixteen editions in a German translation.

Perhaps the association between Mary Ann and Lewes arose not so much on account of their common intellectual interests, but because she needed a man in her life who must be of a certain type. By the time she met him she was interested only in her work, and could not be bothered with the petty domestic details of life. Hence it was Lewes who found lodgings for her on her departure from the Chapmans' house. But she was by no means a sponger; when Lewes became ill and was forbidden to work, after he had found her lodgings, she insisted on doing as much of his work as she could in addition to her own so that he should have something to live on.

At first she had not liked him, but he appealed at last to the maternal streak in her, for he was very poor and often did not get enough to eat. He made no romantic appeal because there was nothing romantic about him, but he had a great soul, and even in the early days of their acquaintance she must have become aware of it.

When he did not recover after his month's rest, she persuaded his doctor to take him on a walking tour, the sovereign Victorian remedy, so often adopted by R. L. Stevenson (q.v.). She would continue to do his work while he walked himself back to health. Lewes returned from his walking exercise much improved.

He returned in June 1853 and by then she was in love with him, and that raised an enormous problem. She could not marry him, because he was married already; his wife had left him, but he kept her and her three sons, and that accounted to a large extent for his poverty. The law of the period precluded a divorce. Lewes, being the man he was, would never ask her to live with him because, owing to the social outlook of the period, such a course would make her a social outcast.

Consequently, by the summer of 1854 Mary Ann was taking the decision into her own hands. She knew that Lewes loved her, and she prepared to go abroad with him.

That led to a great deal of argument between them. Lewes pointed out that he could not afford to keep her and his wife and children as well. She replied that she had money of her own, £120 a year left her by her father and what she made by writing. At last he agreed, and Mary Ann began planning their departure.

The modern reader must now make some effort in order to try and realise exactly what she proposed to face by living with Lewes. All her relations would disapprove of her. No woman would consent to meet her socially. She would be a social embarrassment wherever she went and be quite unable to make new friends except in a very limited circle.

Rather than embarrass Mr. Chapman she resigned the assistant editorship of the *Westminster Review*, though she needed her salary. She said she wanted to take a long holiday.

Then, with her odd-looking little lover, she took passage for Antwerp.

From Belgium they wandered to Germany, perfectly at peace so far, because foreigners accepted them as Mr. and Mrs. G. H. Lewes. When they returned to England people whom they knew would ignore them. Editors would refuse Mary Ann's work if signed because they could not publish the writings of an immoral woman; it was more than their circulations were worth. All her work in future must be either unsigned or signed with a pen-name.

Germany even gave them a triumph. Lewes had been educated there, and he found old friends, and the Germans knew and valued his work. They met Brabant, the father of the Miss Brabant who had married Charles Hennell, and become, in consequence, too busy to finish translating the *Life of Jesus*, which Mary Ann had accomplished. They even met Strauss who wrote the *Life of Jesus* Mary Ann had translated. They spent a long time at Weimar, so that

Lewes could collect the material for his *Life and Works of Goethe*.

It was the year 1854, and Mary Ann was thirty-five, and Lewes thirty-seven.

They continued to Berlin, where living, unfortunately, cost more, for at Weimar their entire expenses had come to £2 6s. a week, and Mary Ann continued to translate Spinoza's *Ethics*, until March 1855, when their wanderings ended and they returned home. Directly she reached Dover she knew the worst; only one letter awaited her. Relations and friends alike had cut her for going away with Lewes.

In April they took rooms in Bayswater, and their eternal money worries began, for Lewes's liabilities had to be met from Mary Ann's income and what they could make by writing. When they could no longer afford Bayswater they lived in one room at East Sheen. But Charles Bray wrote and apologised for his attitude towards her relationship with Lewes, and that made her happy. Her brother and sister refused to recognise her, but it was nice to be friends once more with Charles Bray and his wife.

The story of Mary Ann is now, for a long time, one of grinding poverty. She did not regret the choice she had made, nor grudge the price of it, but the world was to make her pay every penny of the price.

They moved once more, from East Sheen to 8 Park Shot Road, Richmond, sharing the sitting-room as a work-room because they could only afford one. In November of that year (1855) Lewes's *Life and Works of Goethe* appeared in two volumes, price thirty shillings, to be greeted by the critics with unanimous approval. Even an author needs capital in order to make money, but as Lewes possessed none he had sold the first edition of his masterpiece for an outright sum. However, he hoped to make more money on the royalties from a second edition.

But his sons must be sent to school in Germany, and so money vanished. Mary Ann and he gave up eating meat as an economy; no great sacrifice in these days, but an enormous self-denial in the era of Victorian plenty. There was a grim reason behind the sending of Lewes's sons to Germany. The parents of the other boys at their English school had complained about the association of their sons with the sons of a man living in sin. Either Lewes's sons must go or theirs would go. The headmaster had no option but to ask Lewes to take his sons away. Even a personal friend of Mary Ann's refused to teach them for the same reason. There was no choice but to send them abroad at great expense.

Lewes and she set their teeth and looked everywhere for extra work whose proceeds might help to pay school bills. She was forced to keep her work strictly anonymous, for no editor would dare to publish the work of an adulteress if the public guessed her identity. Nobody guessed who wrote her articles, and they improved the circulation of the *Westminster Review*. Lewes's *Goethe* went into a second edition, and they were able to manage a holiday at Ilfracombe, where Lewes went off into an orgy of zoology.

They continued to Tenby, still zoologising, and Mary Ann found herself completely happy. For once she had left her books behind, and her health improved.

She was now thirty-seven, and so far had never published a line of fiction, but there remained in existence an early experiment in fiction, which she had read to Lewes during their honeymoon in Germany. He had urged her to complete it, but at the time she had not taken him seriously. Perhaps his own two novels did not give her much confidence in him as a critic of fiction. Now, after her holiday, she decided to take his advice.

They left Tenby on August 8th, 1856, and returned to Richmond. Mary Ann felt glad to be home.

Having made up her mind to write fiction, she told Mr. Chapman that she did not want to write articles which would give her much trouble. Accordingly, with unconscious irony, he asked her to write an article entitled, "Silly Novels by Lady Novelists". She agreed without a smile. Lewes renewed his encouragement concerning a novel. While she was busy working out details an idea came:

"One morning, as I was thinking what should be the subject of my first story, my thoughts merged themselves into a dreamy doze, and I imagined myself writing a story of which the title was *The Sad Fortunes of the Reverend Amos Barton*. I was soon wide awake again and told G. (Lewes). He said:

" 'Oh, what a capital title,' and from that time I had settled in my mind this should be my first story."

In the result, the Rev. Amos Barton became the first part of her first work of fiction, *Scenes from Clerical Life*.

It is strange, or perhaps significant, that she never doubted the success of her book. Lewes began to be concerned; he watched over her as a mother watches her first child; he feared the psychological consequences to Mary Ann if the book should prove a failure, and begged her not to feel too optimistic. She took no notice and finished her book. Lewes read it, and knew she had triumphed.

Lewes sent it to the house of Blackwood in Edinburgh. His name, of course was known to the firm, and he wrote a discreet letter, saying that, according to his judgment, "such humour, pathos, vivid presentation, and nice observation have not been exhibited (in this style) since the *Vicar of Wakefield*."

The story, naturally, had to be anonymous. No publisher would dare to publish a novel signed by Mary Ann who was living in sin, for no one would read it, and the circulating libraries, for their own sakes, would refuse to handle it. Lewes said the book was written by a friend, and was the beginning of a series, and referred to his friend as "he".

Mr. Blackwood only waited a week before writing:

"I think your friend's reminiscences of clerical life will do." Unfortunately he wanted alterations, like most publishers and editors. Mary Ann, having read the letter, refused point blank, like most female writers, to alter a thing. If Mr. Blackwood refused to publish her work as she wrote it, someone else would publish it.

Lewes counselled calm, and that he should reason with Mr. Blackwood. He wrote that "his clerical friend" refused to alter anything, adding that he could appreciate Mr. Blackwood's hesitation at commissioning a series of which he had only read one example from an unknown author. This sweet reasonableness prevailed. Mr. Blackwood replied that he would forgo alterations, and publish the story in January (1857).

Mary Ann agreed, but the cautious Lewes declared that Mr. Blackwood must not be allowed to go on thinking that the story was written by a clergyman. He therefore wrote again, revealing that the author was not a parson, and insisting that the secret of authorship must still be kept. He stipulated that even his own name, as go-between, should not be mentioned, lest guessers should "jump from me to my friend".

Mary Ann went to work on *Mr. Gilfil's Love Story*, the next in the series, a story her father had told her, a somewhat melodramatic affair, with a dagger in it. Mr. Blackwood made *Amos Barton* the first feature of the January number of his magazine, and sent Mary Ann a copy, a cheque for fifty guineas, and a letter saying that he had put Amos in the leading position because "his merits well entitle him to it". The letter was long and complimentary, and hinted at book publications after the stories had appeared serially.

"It is a long time," wrote Mr. Blackwood, "since I have read anything so fresh, so humorous, and so touching. The style is capital, conveying so much in so few words."

It became obvious to Mary Ann and Lewes that Mr. Blackwood could not be left for ever doing business with a nameless author. Lewes suggested that she should use her own name, but she refused. She therefore wrote to Mr. Blackwood, ending her letter:

"It will be as well to give you my prospective name, as a crust to throw to the whale in case of curious inquiries: and, accordingly I subscribe myself, best and most sympathising of editors,
"Yours very truly,
"GEORGE ELIOT."

The evolution of her pen name has been described already. She and Lewes went away to Cornwall, where she proposed to work on *Mr. Gilfil's Love Story*. From Cornwall they continued to the Scilly Isles, and there *Mr. Gilfil's Love Story* was finished. There also she heard from her brother Isaac that one of her sister's, Christiana's, daughters had died of typhus and that the other was ill. It is typical of Mary Ann that, although her brother and sister had cut her off when she went to live with Lewes, she replied at once with a sympathetic letter. She and Lewes then left the Scilly Isles for Jersey; they could afford a prolonged holiday by now, though in her case it was a writer's holiday, which means change without stopping work. In Jersey she evolved *Janet's Repentance*, the third of her *Scenes from Clerical Life*.

She finished it, and sent it to Mr. Blackwood, and he became full of alarm. In the course of the story Janet is thrown out into the street by her drunken husband, the vicar has condemned her, and she is "saved" by a Methodist minister. Mr. Blackwood's magazine circulated largely among the clergy, and one cannot help sympathising with him.

He wrote to Mary Ann desiring alterations and she replied by asking for the story back and refusing to continue the series. Realising that Mary Ann had increased his circulation, he gave way. *Janet's Repentance* was to be published as written, but Mary Ann declined to write any more *Scenes from Clerical Life*. She had become convinced of her power as a novelist, and she considered Mr. Blackwood unsympathetic. His magazine took no harm from *Janet's Repentance*; on the contrary, the sales increased once more.

Mary Ann and he remained friends. He published *Scenes from Clerical Life* in two volumes, and sent her £120 for the book rights. She proposed now to write a novel, and agreed to let him have the first option on it. On October 22nd, 1857, she began to write *Adam Bede*.

If, as had been alleged by all and sundry, Mary and Lewes were wicked, they did not flee as the wicked flee when no man pursueth; on the contrary, they began to flourish like the green bay tree. Lewes's *Life of Goethe* was in its third edition, his *History of Philosophy* had succeeded, and Mr. Blackwood was going to publish his *Physiology of Common Life*. Mary Ann had become famous through *Scenes from Clerical Life*.

These appeared in book form in 1858, and Charles Dickens wrote a letter of congratulation, beginning "My Dear Sir" to the author. He had enough penetration to remark in the course of the letter:

"I should have been strongly disposed, if I had been left to my own devices, to address the said writer as a woman. I have observed what seemed to me such womanly touches in those moving fictions, that the assurance on the title page is insufficient to satisfy me even now. If they originated with no woman, I believe that no man ever before had the art of making himself mentally so like a woman since the world began."

Mary Ann continued with *Adam Bede*, the theme of the book being adapted from a story told her by her aunt, Mrs. Samuel Evans, the wife of her father's younger brother. Mary Ann records:

"We were sitting together one afternoon during her visit to us at Griff—probably in 1839 or 1840, when it occurred to her to tell me how she had visited a condemned criminal—a very ignorant girl, who had murdered her child, and refused to confess; how she had stayed with her, praying through the night, and how the poor creature at last broke out into tears and confessed her crime. My aunt afterwards went with her in the cart to the place of execution."

Before *Adam Bede* was finished, Lewes asked Mr. Blackwood if he preferred to see it in part or wait for completion. Instead of replying Mr. Blackwood came to London and called on Lewes. Mary Ann was present when he arrived, and Lewes introduced her as his wife. Blackwood asked if he could meet "George Eliot". Mary Ann left the room and Lewes followed her. She said he might tell Mr. Blackwood the truth. He swore he would never give away her secret, and she and he became great friends. All he read of *Adam Bede* was the first page. He commented:

"This will do," and the manuscript was packed forthwith.

Mary Ann and Lewes departed for Germany in April (1858) and in Leipzig she finished the second volume of *Adam Bede*. (Those were the days of the three-volume novel totalling about 300,000 words.) They returned to England after five months, and by the end of October she had completed the third volume. Mr. Blackwood said the novel was a masterpiece, and offered her £800 for a four years' copyright. Mary Ann accepted, and wrote on the first page of her manuscript:

"To my dear husband, George Henry Lewes, I give the MS of a work that would never have been written but for the happiness which his love conferred on my life."

Being now not only happy in each other, but successful, in the New Year of 1859 they began house-hunting. In the end they took a house in Wandsworth for seven years. A cheque for £400 arrived from Mr. Blackwood, and on February 6th they moved from Richmond.

When *Adam Bede* appeared, it succeeded from the start and, not unnaturally, the question of the day became:

"Who is 'George Eliot'?"

Mary Ann refused to gratify the world's curiosity.

That year her sister Christiana died of consumption. No one had been more bitter than Christiana about the Mary Ann–Lewes conjunction, but on her death bed she wished to be forgiven. She wrote apologetically, and died shriven as far as Mary Ann could shrive her.

There then occurred one of the most extraordinary hoaxes in the history of literature. A friend in Warwickshire wrote to Mary Ann:

"I want to ask you if you have read *Adam Bede* or the *Scenes from Clerical Life*, and whether you know that the author is Mr. Liggins? He is the son of a baker, of no mark at all in his town, so that it is possible you may not have heard of him. . . . You know he calls himself 'George Eliot'! It sounds strange to hear the *Westminster* doubting whether he is a woman, when here he is so well known. But I am glad it has mentioned him. They say he gets no profit out of *Adam Bede* and gives it all freely to Blackwood, which is a shame."

Mary Ann sent this to Mr. Blackwood with some enjoyment.

A Mr. Bracebridge, J.P., of Warwickshire, had started the story. Perceiving the obvious, that the author of *Adam Bede* must be a Warwickshire "man", Mr. Bracebridge set out to find him, and fastened the authorship on the obscure Liggins, who existed. The news appeared in the papers, and Mr. Liggins became famous. Being usually so drunk that he never knew what he did, he gave no convincing explanation to visitors as to how he wrote the book, but accepted the title of author and complained that Mr. Blackwood never paid him for his work. Mr. Blackwood received rude letters from the public but remained calm. Publishers, like authors, receive so many rude letters from the public.

Mary Ann did not remain calm, especially when the public began to subscribe for a testimonial to Mr. Liggins to recompense him for the alleged stinginess of his publisher. She wrote to Mr. Blackwood, asking him to send a letter to *The Times* denying that Mr. Liggins had written *Adam Bede*. Mr. Black-wood replied that it would be better for her to admit the authorship of the book, especially as the Rev. H. Anders, rector of Kirby, had already stated in a letter published in *The Times*:

"The author of *Scenes from Clerical Life* and *Adam Bede* is Mr. Joseph Liggins of Nuneaton, Warwickshire."

Finally, Lewes, who dealt with all Mary Ann's troubles, dealt with this one. He wrote to the Rev. H. Anders, and saw Mr. Bracebridge. The rector admitted he was wrong, and Mr. Bracebridge set out to contradict himself.

But Charles Bray and his wife, Mary Ann's friends, believed in Liggins and Mary Ann revealed her authorship of *Adam Bede* to Charles, swearing him to secrecy. The secret then leaked out, and her anonymity disappeared for ever.

Reaction now set in. Mary Ann, who had never entertained the faintest doubt concerning *Adam Bede*'s merits asked herself:

"Shall I ever write another book as true as *Adam Bede*?" and added:

"The weight of the future presses upon me." However, Mr. Blackwood sent her a present of a dog from Edinburgh. Its name was "Pug" and it cheered her up. She began to work on a new novel, called in the first instance *Sister Maggie*, and finally *The Mill on the Floss*. There is much in the character of Maggie Tulliver which recalls Mary Ann herself. The book went on apace, partly because Lewes took over the house-keeping, and saw that she could devote herself entirely to the business of writing. He let his own work go, in the spirit of Captain Reece, commander of the *Mantelpiece*:

> " *My own convenience counts as nil ;*
> *It is my duty, and I will.*"

Perhaps Mary Ann never realised, in spite of the dedication on page 1 of the MS. of *Adam Bede*, how much she owed to the love, unselfishness, and self-suppression of George Lewes.

She finished *The Mill on the Floss* in March 1860, and the MS. bore the dedication:

"To my beloved husband, George Henry Lewes, I give this MS. of my third book, written in the sixth year of our life together at Holly Lodge, South Field, Wandsworth."

Lewes had done well by the book, for, among other services, he acted as her literary agent. He had arranged for Mr. Blackwood to pay her £2,000 on account of four thousand sets of the three volumes, with Harpers, of New York, to pay £300 for the American copyright, and with Williams and Norgate to sell the German reprint to Tauchnitz for £100.

On the strength of these triumphs the happy couple departed to Italy, visiting Rome, Florence, and Bologna, and Mary Ann became the prey of a new idea and insisted on returning home at once to develop it. At this point, one of Lewes's sons impinged on the scene: Charles had ended his schooldays, and was entering the Post Office. He must live at Holly Lodge, and break up the solitude *à deux* which existed there. Fortunately Charles and Mary Ann became great friends, and harmony continued at Holly Lodge. Charles passed his Post Office examination, and Mary Ann had her portrait painted by Lawrence, and planned two novels; one a fifteenth century historical romance set in Florence, the other *Silas Marner*. The ever faithful Mr. Blackwood approved her scheme—by now he knew better than to oppose her in the slightest degree. They found Holly Lodge inconvenient, and moved first to a flat in Harewood Square, which turned out to be worse than Holly Lodge, and in December (1860) to 16 Blandford Square. There she finished *Silas Marner* in March 1861. It made one volume instead of three, and Mr. Blackwood considered it sombre, but the subscription for it reached 5,500 copies, and Mary Ann rejoiced and departed with Lewes for Florence to gather material for her historical romance.

They returned in June, and Mary Ann started on *Romola*, which she found very hard going. Sometimes she gave it up, and sometimes she tore it up; sometimes it made her ill, but she always returned to it, because, periodically, the devil puts it into the heart of every author to write something for which he, or she, is unsuited. *Romola* marked the beginning of the downward curve in Mary Ann's graph of successful writing. In her previous novels she had written of what she knew and had lived; *Romola* was largely a matter of research work.

Increasing recognition by leading lights of literature, Browning, Trollope, Wilkie Collins—soothed Mary Ann's outraged social feelings, but *Romola* was not finished by the end of 1861.

On New Year's Day, 1862, she set herself doggedly to make a new attempt on this historical nightmare, for as such it had begun to appear to her. Before the month of January was out *Romola* had become the reason for a perfectly staggering offer. It is of the nature of publishers to lure profitable authors away from other publishers if they can. That month Mr. Smith, of Smith Elder & Co., a publisher of note, went to see Mary Ann, was received by Lewes as her agent, and made a remarkable suggestion. He said he would like to publish Mary Ann's next novel, and would pay £10,000 for the right of serialising it in the *Cornhill Magazine* and the book rights. (It was Mr. Smith who had founded *Cornhill*, and appointed Thackeray (q.v.) as its first editor.)

But Mr. Smith wished to begin the serialisation of the novel in the May issue of *Cornhill*, and as Mary Ann was just beginning it all over again that was impossible. Mr. Smith replied that he would allow her more time and pay £7,000 and Mary Ann accepted the proposal, realising that now she would have to finish *Romola* at any cost.

She fled to Englefield Green, in the hope that change would bring inspiration, and continued to Dorking. In September she appeared at Littlehampton, still struggling with *Romola*. She had not finished it by the end of 1862, but the end came in June 1863.

She and Lewes took a holiday in the Isle of Wight, and then they began home-seeking once more. They wanted a fairly large house because Thornton and Bertie had to be thought of. Thornton and Bertie were Lewes's wife's sons by another man, but Lewes had accepted responsibility for them. He was that kind of husband, and Mary Ann, in her quaint way, admired him for being that kind of husband. On the other hand, it annoyed her to think that Lewes, by condoning his wife's misconduct, had put divorcing her out of the realm of possibility, so that he could never marry Mary Ann.

Consequently, having contributed towards their education, she desired that they should be exported. Thornton and Bertie agreed, being adventurous youths, and so they were exported to Natal. Charles, of the Post Office, conveniently became engaged. The new house was called The Priory, and Lewes became ill, and Mary Ann suddenly decided to be a poet, her poem to be called *The Spanish Gipsy*. Her excursion into poetry can only be called regrettable; the form was the form of Milton, but the execution was the execution of Mary Ann.

Lewes encouraged her in this plan to produce a poetic drama, because he loved her. But although, in January 1865, she recorded that "the last quarter has made an epoch for me by the fact that, for the first time in my serious authorship, I have written verse", the result is far from epochal.

In 1865, Lewes was appointed editor of the new *Fortnightly Review*, and proceeded to give a celebration party. The result of this party demonstrates the so-called moral outlook of the Victorians. Mary Ann, with all a woman's delight in a party, looked forward to it with exceeding great joy. At the beginning of her association with Lewes she would have known better than to give a party, even if she could have afforded it, because no one would have accepted an invitation. Much had happened since then, and she and Lewes were known to be famous. Surely now a party could be given successfully?

They hired a band, and servants, and she chose a new frock. People accepted invitations, and on the great night wax candles shed their light within The Priory. One hundred and fifty invitations had been sent out; fourteen guests appeared. Mary Ann and Lewes braved it out, and Mary Ann realised that, in spite of her fame, in the eyes of society she was still a whore.

She began doggedly to write *Felix Holt* and Lewes made a success of the *Fortnightly Review*. She and he holidayed in Holland, and continued to Spain for the sake of that unfortunate poetic drama *The Spanish Gipsy*. When the drama was finished they visited Germany, so that Mary Ann could get away from England and people who refused to be seen at her house, and came back inevitably to London, and went on with *Felix Holt* as though no one had ever bilked her invitations to a party.

At this stage Lewes was a sick man, and so Herbert Spencer, who had once nearly loved Mary Ann, took him for the Victorian cure, a walking tour, in Surrey. There they called on a Mrs. Cross, who lived in style at Weybridge, and Herbert Spencer, perhaps as a return for never having quite loved Mary Ann, persuaded Mrs. Cross to receive her. John Cross, Mrs. Cross's eldest son, in New York City, who admired Mary

Ann's books beyond measure, heard of this and was glad. On his return to England he would be able to meet his admired author.

Meanwhile Mary Ann continued, professionally, from strength to strength. She worked for three years on *The Spanish Gipsy*, and it only shows what love will do when we realise that Lewes encouraged her to finish it. Reviewers disagreed with him and hurt Mary Ann very much, so much that Lewes felt obliged to cut the reviews of *The Spanish Gipsy* out of such papers as she saw. She survived the hurt, and in 1869 began work on *Middlemarch*.

In the spring of 1869 she and Lewes visited Italy and here met Mrs. Cross's eldest daughter on her honeymoon. Later Mrs. Cross and her son John appeared in Rome, and called on Mary Ann and Lewes at their hotel.

John Cross has left his impression of Mary Ann: of the musical tones of her voice, her auburn-brown hair, her grey-blue eyes, and her finely-formed, thin, transparent hands. Then the moment passed and Mary Ann and Lewes left Rome, and John Cross did not meet them again until the following August, at Weybridge.

This is all very important because, ultimately, Mary Ann was to marry John Cross.

Early in 1870, she and Lewes journeyed to Berlin once more, and the visit developed into a triumphal progress, partly on account of Lewes's *Life and Works of Goethe*, partly on account of Mary Ann's novels. On their return to London they found themselves at last accepted socially. On Sundays they were open to receive everyone, and everyone called. Whoever else called, there was always John Cross worshipping in the background while Mary Ann held what amounted to a salon. Every year added its quota of leaves to her garland of laurel. *Middlemarch* eclipsed its predecessors in celebrity, and by the end of 1874, 20,000 copies had been sold at the price of one guinea each.

And then death, the stealthy-footed, began to abridge life.

Thornton had died, and so had Dickens, Mary Ann's friend, and in 1875 Bertie died. On the other hand Lewes's health had improved, and Charles was the father of a girl. Mary Ann, beset by publishers, who will never let a best-selling novelist rest, produced another novel, *Daniel Deronda*, which is still topical, because Daniel departed, not to the lions' den, but to found a Jewish community in Palestine. The curve in the graph of her achievement continued to droop, for the novel is propaganda and does not reach the height of *Adam Bede* and *The Mill on the Floss*, but it sold by the thousand copies.

So, on the profits of all these best sellers, Mary Ann and Lewes became almost "landed gentry" by acquiring "The Heights", Witley, Surrey. This was a fine house and, instead of leaving it to George, she furnished and decorated the place herself. They were now "carriage people" with a spanking pair of greys to draw the carriage. Mary Ann's Sunday parties became much sought after, and inevitably, as at "The Priory", John Cross appeared at them whenever he could. Among those calling at "The Heights" we find their neighbours, Sir Henry and Lady Holland, the du Mauriers, the Allinghams, and the Tennysons. Mary Ann and Lewes had arrived socially as well as professionally.

But already John Cross had noted that "in our drives in the neighbourhood of Witley Mr. Lewes used sometimes to be seized suddenly with cramping pains. I think he was himself aware that something was seriously wrong, but the moment the pain ceased the extraordinary buoyancy of his spirits returned. Nothing but death could quench that bright flame."

Death was to quench it very soon. The doctors took an optimistic view of the sixty-year-old patient's health, but on November 25th, 1878, Mary Ann wrote to Mr. Blackwood that Lewes continued sadly ill and that she was absorbed in nursing him; on November 28th he died.

The story of Mary Ann now draws to its close. She wanted to die after Lewes died, and refused to see her friends, but one of them told her that she must finish Lewes's book, *The Problems of Life and Mind*, and that gave her new energy. Also, there was John Cross.

In spite of being twenty years her junior he longed to comfort her. She wrote to him in February 1879 that she needed his affection, and would see him in a week or two. A fortnight after he had received the letter she invited him to call on her, and found that she could not exist without him. Lewes's book had been completed; she was busy on a book of her own for Mr. Blackwood; Lewes had always seen to the details of her life; Lewes had left her; and here was John Cross ready and eager to take his place and free her from all the petty worries of a working life.

Their wedding took place in the spring of 1880, at St. George's, Hanover Square; the choice of this sacred edifice demonstrates that Mary Ann had indeed arrived from the social point of view.

She did not love John Cross, but he wanted to marry her, and she needed someone to remove small annoyances from her path. Also she longed passionately to be married, to have the status of a married woman. It was the one thing that so far had eluded her, and now she had it.

They honeymooned on the Continent, and returned to Witley. December 1880 found them in No. 4 Cheyne Walk, Chelsea. Mary Ann had been ill, but recovered and plunged into the social delights of London. Towards the end of that month she became ill again, with laryngitis, said the doctor, but it proved to be something more serious. She died on December 22nd, and was buried, at her desire, in unconsecrated ground, next to George Henry Lewes.

John Cross had only been married to her for seven months, but she had given him immortality. She and Lewes had been faithful to one another for twenty-five years.

Mary Ann is a difficult person to understand at this distance of time, especially as the modern generation finds the attitude of hers towards her association with Lewes quite incomprehensible. If she were alive today no one would care whether she was married to Lewes or not. She would take her natural position as a great writer irrespective of her private life.

That she was essentially feminine there is no doubt. In spite of her love for Lewes, the admiration of John Cross, twenty years younger than herself, appealed to her. Her marriage to him gave her great satisfaction; after the ceremony in St. George's, Hanover Square, she was "as good as any other woman". Nor, although she once refused to go to church with her father, did she kick against being married in a church, though she refused to be buried in consecrated ground away from Lewes.

She regarded herself as an aesthetic teacher. She held that such teaching was "the highest of all teaching, because it deals with life in its highest complexity. But if it ceases to be purely aesthetic—if it lapses anywhere from the picture to the diagram —it becomes the most offensive of all teaching."

That was the standard she set for herself.

As a novelist, whether or no she lived up to her own standard, she will always rank among the greatest of the English school. Oddly enough, her most successful novels, *Adam Bede*, *Silas Marner*, *Felix Holt*, *Middlemarch*, and *Daniel Deronda* had as their theme that love without marriage or marriage without love is equally selfish and desecrating. Yet in her own life she loved Lewes without marrying him. There she demonstrates a feminine inconsistency which never seems to have occurred to her.

She wrote of the surroundings in which she was born, of middle-class farmers and tradesmen in the Midlands, with a penetrating observation which has scarcely been surpassed. The dialogue in her novels is brilliant, and yet there is hardly a good letter among the vast mass of hers which survive.

We may sum her up as a brilliant personality, a dogged worker, a superb craftswoman, with a heart of gold, and enough of the small human frailties to save her from an inhuman perfection.

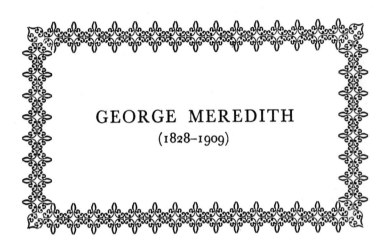

GEORGE MEREDITH
(1828–1909)

GEORGE MEREDITH

From the canvas by G. F. Watts now in the
National Portrait Gallery

GEORGE MEREDITH

(1828–1909)

LIKE DICKENS, George Meredith suffered from an in-feriority complex, but it did not make him abounding and suffocating as it made Dickens. Meredith was a great aristocrat in his own way, and Dante Gabriel Rossetti used his handsome head as a model for Christ in the picture "Mary Magdalene at the gate of Simon the Pharisee". No painter would have dreamed of using Dickens's head as a model for Christ, even though, like Meredith, he wore a beard.

Meredith, an aristocrat by temperament if not by birth, hated and concealed the fact that his father and grandfather were tailors, or rather naval outfitters. This *motif* of a young man's despising his tailoring parentage occurs in Meredith's novel, *Evan Harrington*. Not until after Meredith's death was the name of his birthplace known; he was born at Portsmouth on February 12th, 1828. Indeed, he made so much mystery about his birth and parentage that he was rumoured to be the illegitimate son of a royal naval officer.

If it had not been for a psycho-pathological attitude towards them, he need not have despised his ancestors.

Meredith's grandfather, Melchizedek Meredith, cut a splendid figure in Portsmouth and the neighbourhood, tailor or no tailor. He was a tall, handsome man, and lived at 73 High Street, Portsmouth, where Meredith was born. Mel-chizedek married a woman as handsome as himself—no doubt he could pick and choose—and they had two sons and five daughters. As he prospered he became, on account of his personal qualities, for in those days a great gulf stretched between tradesmen and gentlemen, on visiting terms with county families. He also hunted, and held a commission in the Portsmouth Yeomanry Cavalry. Like so many splendid people, he spent lavishly, and in consequence his business suffered, and also his finances. He died in 1814 at the early age of fifty-one.

There remained then in the family house, No. 73 High Street, his widow, his youngest daughter and his son, Augustus Urmston Meredith, aged seventeen. His other son had died. Mrs. Meredith carried on the business during her son's minority. In due time he married Miss Jane Eliza Macnamara, a childhood sweetheart whose parents lived chose by. Augustus had inherited his father's good looks, and Jane Eliza was a beautiful girl; and these things account for the handsome head and dignified bearing of their son, George Meredith. He was born in the home of his father and grandfather and christened on April 9th, 1828, in St. Thomas's Church. Seven months later his grandmother died, and the naval outfitting business passed entirely to his father.

Meredith was an only child, and has described his childhood as unhappy. There is no evidence to show why he should have been unhappy, at any rate up to the age of five. In his fifth year his mother died, aged thirty-one. A grown-up cousin, Mary Burbey, who lived opposite, did what she could to take the place of his mother, and an aunt, Mrs. Ellis, also kept an eye on him when she happened to be in the neighbourhood.

His father, like his grandfather, found friends in a more exclusive society than that of Portsmouth's commercial circle. Augustus Meredith inherited his father's, Melchizedek's, taste for spending money, especially on entertaining, and, between these extravagant habits and neglect of his business, found himself in difficulties over money. He was a good father, if an unsuccessful one. He and George never got on together, in spite of the fact that Augustus went almost to the length of spoiling him; oddly enough, the same difficult relationship existed between Meredith and his own son, whom he began by spoiling.

Meredith's schooldays began when he reached the age of nine and entered St. Paul's School, Southsea. At this period he was a good-looking boy with blue-grey eyes and curly hair, better dressed than the other boys who lived in his streets, and attended a less fashionable school. They considered him stuck-up and called him "Gentleman Georgy". Like most only children, who at home are a great deal with grown-ups, he felt a certain contempt for other boys of his age, who seem childish and uninteresting to the mentally older only child.

Besides, as his after-life demonstrated, he *was* superior to them, and the thoroughbred can hardly be expected to feel unconscious of his merits.

In 1841 Augustus Meredith married a second time, sold his Portsmouth business, which continued to languish, and departed to try again in London, where eventually he set up in St. James's Street. He sent his son to school in the country. Meredith's departure from Portsmouth caused him no pang, or at any rate no additional pang. He had pangs enough owing to his sensitive temperament which led him eternally to suffer from imaginary slights.

Augustus Meredith succeeded no better in London than he had succeeded in Portsmouth, but Meredith inherited a small legacy from his mother, and in 1842 his trustee sent him to be educated at the Moravian School, at Neuwied, in Germany. There he delighted in the German way of life. Neuwied is on the Rhine, and the romantic Rhineland scenery may have had something to do with his affection for Germany. He was fourteen years old when he entered the Moravian School, an age when the imagination is easily captivated, particularly in the case of an intelligent, highly-strung boy.

Meredith remained at Neuwied for two years without seeing his own country, returning to England in 1844. He was then sixteen. Nobody knows what happened to him for the next two years, but in 1846 he became an articled clerk in a solicitor's office. He was now a ward in Chancery, and the legacy from his mother enabled him to study law.

Meredith must have been an attractive youth, and the solicitor to whom he was articled, Richard Stephen Charnock, seems to have taken a fancy to him, since he introduced Meredith to his friends, for the most part writers and artists. Among them were Edward Peacock, son of the novelist Thomas Love Peacock, and Mrs. Nicholls. Charnock and his friends produced a manuscript magazine called *The Monthly Observer*, and Meredith's first published poem appeared in it. Later the poem (Chillianwallah) was published in *Chambers's Journal* for July 7th, 1849.

In that year Augustus Meredith departed with his wife (he had married a second time, his bride being Matilda Buckett, his housekeeper) to South Africa and started business again in

Cape Town. Thus Meredith, at the age of twenty-one, found himself alone in London, and took cheap lodgings in Pimlico. He was very poor, for his mother's legacy had dwindled by now. The temptations of a young man alone in London are many, but he had already formed the habit of taking the tremendous country walks which remained a joy to him all his life until age and infirmity put an end to them. His walks always took him through Surrey, the county in which the majority of his days were to be spent. By now he had abandoned law and chosen literature as a profession.

A companion on his walks was Edward Peacock, and at Peacock's rooms Meredith met his sister, Mary Ellen Nicholls, a beautiful widow thirty years of age. She had married Lieutenant Nicholls, R.N., in 1844, and four months after the marriage her husband was drowned at sea, leaving her a widow and the mother of his posthumous daughter.

Either because Meredith had met few women, or because of the proverbial charm of a beautiful young widow he fell violently in love with Mary Ellen, who was nine years older than he. She refused him six times, perhaps because his income scarcely existed, but the handsome Meredith as a young man must have seemed practically irresistible, for their wedding took place at St. George's, Hanover Square, on August 9th, 1849.

Fortunately Meredith received about this time a second legacy from another relation, and so he took Mary Ellen to the Continent, returning in November, when they stayed with her father in John Street, Adelphi. The marriage, though it was to end in failure, started favourably enough. For one thing, both Meredith and his wife wrote poetry, which provided a common interest. But a successful marriage can only be founded on a home, and the Merediths had no home. Either they stayed with Mary Ellen's father, or lived in lodgings or boarding houses. They spent a considerable period at The Limes, Weybridge, inhabited by a Mrs. Macirone, the widow of a colonel. She and her two lovely daughters had literary friends, among them Bulwer Lytton and Tom Taylor. Through Taylor, Meredith met Sir Alexander Duff Gordon and her ladyship, who also lived at Weybridge. Their eight-year-old daughter Janet became very fond of Meredith and he adored her. He was introduced to Charles Dickens (q.v.), and a number of his poems appeared in *Household Words*, which Dickens was then editing, or "conducting" as he preferred to call it.

Meredith's first book, *Poems*, 1851, appeared at his own expense, in the summer of that year. He made no money out of it, but the reviews were reasonably appreciative. The poems included "Love in the Valley". William Michael Rossetti, reviewing the book in the *Critic*, wrote:

"We do not expect ever quite to enrol Mr. Meredith among the demi-gods or heroes . . . but we shall not cease to look for his renewed appearance with hope, and to hail it with extreme pleasure, so long as he may continue to produce poems equal to the best in this first volume." Charles Kingsley reviewed the poems still more favourably in *Fraser's Magazine* later in the year. However, the reviews did not please Meredith who, all his life, complained, groundlessly on the whole, that reviewers never did him justice.

It was pleasant enough to live in the Weybridge of those days, with Thomas Love Peacock, Mary Ellen's father, living just across the river at Lower Halliford. His wife died in 1852, and in the following year Meredith and his wife left Mrs. Macirone and went to live with Peacock. In his house Meredith's son, Arthur Gryffydh Meredith, was born on June 13th, 1853. Sharing a home with in-laws is never satisfactory. Peacock was sixty-eight and set in his ways, and the highly-strung Meredith cannot have been easy to live with. Peacock solved the problem by renting a small house called Vine Cottage on the opposite side of Halliford Green to his own for his son-in-law and daughter to live in. Here Meredith played cricket with his step-daughter and her friends and finished *The Shaving of Shagpat*, an Oriental story with a family resemblance to *The Arabian Nights*, published by Chapman & Hall at the end of 1856. It was unsuccessful, though the reviews praised the book. "George Eliot" (q.v.), reviewing it, called it a work of genius.

In that year and the following one the Merediths spent much time at Seaford. Maurice Fitzgerald, nephew of Edward Fitzgerald, a great friend of Meredith's, stayed here, too. They all lodged with the village carpenter, whose wife was a remarkable cook, and Meredith loved his meals. He wrote *Farina: a Legend of Cologne* there and it appeared not very gloriously in the autumn of 1857. "George Eliot" felt, on this occasion, disappointed, possibly because the book was written in the affected style which handicaps many of Meredith's novels.

By this time his marriage showed signs of breaking up. He and his wife were both gifted, highly strung, and domineering. They lived at far too close quarters in lodgings and quarrelled frequently. In 1858 the end came when Mary Ellen left Seaford for Capri with a painter named Henry Wallis. Marriage had become so unendurable for her that she abandoned her five-year-old son, who remained with Meredith. She died in 1861, in her forty-first year.

The failure of his marriage wounded Meredith deeply. That this should happen to him, the intellectual aristocrat, could hardly be borne. He wanted his life to be lived in the grand manner and there is nothing very grand for a husband in his wife's eloping with someone else because she cannot endure him any longer. Besides, Henry Wallis had found Mary Ellen alone at Seaford and in debt. The circumstances of her departure were far from glorious from Meredith's point of view.

Thus, at the age of thirty, he found himself wifeless, with a small son in his care. For the time being he hated all women, and devoted himself during the next few years to little Arthur, whom he adored and spoiled just as he, in his own childhood, had been adored and spoiled. The process succeeded no better with Arthur than it had with his father, for Meredith and his son were to become estranged, just as Meredith and his father had become estranged.

He took lodgings in Hobury Street, Chelsea, and there finished his novel *The Ordeal of Richard Feverel*, already begun under the title of *The Fair Frankincense*. Chapman & Hall published it in 1859. *The Ordeal of Richard Feverel* is a novel of characters and the results of their actions, and is the first of the true Meredithian line of novels. His previous books derived largely from a youthful passion for *The Arabian Nights*. He had begun, so to speak, in glorious Technicolor, but his success was to come through the medium of sober black and white. As seems to have been the custom with Victorian novelists, for Dickens and Thackeray did exactly the same thing, the characters in the novel are taken from life. "Adrian Harley" is Meredith's friend, Maurice Fitzgerald; "Mrs. Berry" is Mrs. Ockenden, the wife of the carpenter with whom he lodged in Seaford; and "Lady Feverel" resembles in her circumstances Meredith's first wife.

The country in this novel is the country round Weybridge and Shepperton. "Raynham Abbey" was taken from Woburn Park, Addlestone, and Farmer Blaize's farm, "Belthorpe", from Ham Farm. The very name "Belthorpe" may have been adapted from Thorp, a village not far from Weybridge, between Chertsey and Virginia Water. Richard met Lucy at the old lock at Shepperton.

Lucy in *Richard Feverel* is the most appealing of all Meredith's heroines. Few of Lucy's admirers can forgive Meredith for killing her, and *The Times* reviewer, who gave the book a three-column review, wrote, with reason, that the author deserved to be haunted by the ghost of his most beautiful creation. The incredible "sweetness" of Lucy cloys the palate of the modern reader, and her patience with the ridiculous prig, Richard Feverel, exasperates him, but the love-scene between Richard and Lucy on the river bank creates the most appealing picture of young love achieved by any novelist.

Though *Richard Feverel* as a novel is purer than the driven snow, the *Spectator* said it had a low ethical tone, and so Mudie's Library, now extinct, which depended on the subscriptions of Victorian mammas, refused to circulate it.

In the year of *Richard Feverel's* publication (1859), Meredith and his son took lodgings at Esher. Here he found the Duff Gordons, whom he had met at Weybridge, once more. The circumstances were dramatic. Let Janet Duff Gordon (afterwards Janet Ross) tell the story herself:

"I was riding down to the station to meet my father, as I did every day (she was sixteen at the time) when a small boy fell in the road just in front of my horse. I jumped off, picked him up, and he made heroic efforts not to cry.

"'Papa says little men ought not to cry,' he said, stifling his sobs. I asked him where his father lived, and he pointed to a cottage with a garden in front, where I knew lodgings were to be had. Telling the groom to ride on, I led my horse with one hand and the little boy with the other, and rang. A gentleman came out, kissed the child, and then looked hard at me.

"'Are you not Lady Duff Gordon's daughter?' he asked, and before the answer was out of my mouth he clasped me in his arms, exclaiming:

"'Oh, my Janet! Don't you know me? I'm your Poet.'

"Meredith had left Weybridge before we moved from London to Esher, and though all his friends, particularly Tom Taylor, had tried to find out where he and his baby boy were, he seemed to have vanished into space. He did not know we lived at Esher, and at once declared he would come and live near us.

"I was obliged to ride off to the station to meet my father, but on our way home we stopped and told him to come to dinner. Great was the joy at having found our friend again. Next morning I joined him in searching for a cottage, and we found one, fit retreat for a poet, standing alone on Copsham Common, near the fir woods behind Claremont Park. There Meredith installed himself, and when he went to London twice a week, being reader to Messrs. Chapman & Hall, he brought his little son Arthur to me, and I taught him German. We used to take long walks together. The Black Pool in the fir woods, where a stately heron was often to be found, was one of our favourite haunts. My Poet would recite poetry, or talk about his novels. . . ."

Janet Duff Gordon became to Meredith what most people would call his Egeria. As not one per cent of them would know whether the original Egeria was a patent medicine, an article of male attire worn by the Romans, or a classical lady of no reputation, it may be explained that Egeria was an ancient Italian goddess of Spring, one of the Camenæ, often consulted by Numa Pompilius; hence the modern meaning of Egeria: a female adviser. She continues:

"*Evan Harrington* (which was first called 'He Would be a Gentleman') was *my* novel because Rose Jocelyn was myself. (Sir Frank and Lady Jocelyn were my father and mother, and Miss Current was Miss Louisa Courtenay, a very old friend of my parents who often stayed with us at Esher.) With the magnificent impertinence of sixteen I would interrupt Meredith, exclaiming:

"'No, I should never have said it like that'; or 'I should not have done so.' A young Irish retriever, Peter, which I was breaking in and afterwards gave to little Arthur, was immortalised in the pages of the novel at my special request."

So masterpieces are written, or, at any rate, sometimes.

Sir Francis Burnand, who was introduced to Meredith by Maurice Fitzgerald, has left this picture of him as he appeared when living at Esher:

"George strode towards us . . . he never merely walked, never lounged, he strode, he took giant strides. He had on a soft, shapeless wide-awake, a sad-coloured flannel shirt with low, open collar turned over a brilliant scarlet neckerchief tied in a loose sailor's knot; no waistcoat; knickerbockers, grey stockings, and the most serviceable laced boots which evidently meant business in pedestrianism; crisp, curly, brownish hair ignorant of a parting; a fine brow, quick, observant eyes, greyish if I remember; beard and moustache a trifle lighter than the hair. A splendid head, a memorable personality. Then his sense of humour, his cynicism, and his absolutely boyish enjoyment of mere fun, of any pure and simple absurdity. His laugh was something to hear: it was of short duration, but it was a roar."

Meredith was happy at Copsham Cottage. There he wrote *Evan Harrington*, *Modern Love*, *Sandra Belloni*, and *Poems of the English Roadside*. On Copsham Common congregated gypsies, beggars, and other odds and ends of humanity, and Meredith knew them all. He used his knowledge of them in *The Adventures of Harry Richmond* when he came to write the book.

Through contributing to *Once a Week* he had already met Dante Gabriel Rossetti, and through him Swinburne. The Duff Gordons brought him into contact with Mrs. Norton, who inspired his novel *Diana of the Crossways*, Millais, and G. F. Watts. In 1862 he formed a close friendship with William Hardman, also a great walker, a Lancashire man. He became editor of the *Morning Post* in 1872 and was knighted in 1885. Meredith immortalised him as "Blackburn Tuckham" in *Beauchamp's Career*. Like Meredith, Hardman wore a beard and moustache and was addicted to knickerbockers: a large, hearty, Victorian male.

Hardman has left a charming description of a short walking tour with Meredith in 1862.

He and Meredith dined at the Copsham cottage, and set out at seven p.m. If they could not find a night's lodging at Mickleham they proposed to continue to Burford Bridge. Hardman carried all his toilet articles and nightwear in the pockets of his shooting jacket. As these could hardly contain the Victorian nightshirt, perhaps he slept in his day shirt. Meredith wore a rucksack, in which he had stowed besides his gear *Murray's Handbook to Surrey* and "some capital brandy".

There was a certain boyish make-believe between these two bearded men in the thirties, who delighted to play at bandits. They did not call one another by their names. Hardman was "Tuck" and Meredith "Robin". They posed as Robin Hood and one of his merry men in the greenwood. They walked slowly after their good dinner, and sang and made rhymes as they walked. When they reached Mickleham it was dark. The landlady at the inn could put them up, and while she prepared their rooms they strolled out and listened to the nightingales. "Robin," appropriately enough, recited Keats's "Ode to a Nightingale". They returned to the inn, drank Meredith's brandy with soda water, and went to bed at eleven; as their rooms "communicated by a passage", they lay shouting to one another and joking for an hour or so.

They rose at seven a.m., inspected the churchyard, breakfasted on eggs, kidneys, and chops, and resumed their walk. They passed by Burford Bridge, continued to Dorking, proceeded towards Guildford, and ate a luncheon of beer and bread and cheese at Shere. The afternoon's walk took them by Combe Bottom and Newlands Corner back to Guildford, and they ordered a cold dinner. "Robin" bought the *Spectator* for May 24th, 1862, at the station. It contained a very unpleasant article on his *Poems* and *Modern Love*. After dinner they walked on to Godalming. At a small inn near Milford they found beds. They ordered tea, but could not refrain from strolling to a hill on a wild common nearby. At nine they were more than ready for bed, having been on foot for twelve hours.

The next morning was Sunday. They rose at seven, and

had coffee, chops, and unlimited bread and butter for breakfast. The landlady charged them 3*s*. 6*d*. each for supper, bed,
and breakfast (with chops). Hardman adds:

"We gave sixpence to the little maid who waited on us,
and she was greatly pleased."

They set off by Thursley to the Devil's Punch Bowl, where
they lay on the ground and smoked. Reaching Haslemere
by one o'clock, they knocked at the White Horse and had
"a cut at the family dinner, a breast of veal, washed down by
copious draughts of the best pale ale Meredith and I had ever
tasted". They lingered till three o'clock, and then left for
Godalming in a four-wheeled chaise to catch the five-fifteen
p.m. train, as there was none from Haslemere till seven-
twenty p.m. Hardman dropped Meredith at Esher and
continued to London alone. Such were the simple Victorian
pleasures of strong men, in days when a little maid felt very
pleased to receive a tip of sixpence from two of them. There
was nothing Meredith liked better than rambling on foot
over his beloved Surrey.

Meanwhile, *Evan Harrington* had appeared serially in *Once a
Week* in 1860 and been published in a three-volume edition
in 1861. The story is not convincing, though Meredith introduced his father, three aunts, and his grandparents into it,
besides, as we have seen, Janet Duff Gordon, her parents,
and their family friend, Mrs. Courtenay.

In the summer of 1861 he went abroad with his little son,
Arthur. They went by Ostend and the Rhine to Zurich and
continued through Austria and Italy, returning home by way
of Paris. During the whole of this journey Meredith looked
after his son personally, though nothing can be more exasperat-
ing to an intelligent man than the need of bringing himself
down, day in and day out, to the mental level of a small boy.

Modern Love and *Poems of the English Countryside* appeared in
the spring of 1862 without advancing greatly Meredith's
reputation. The *Spectator* for May 24th of that year, a copy
of which, it will be remembered, he bought at Guildford
railway station while on the walking tour with Hardman,
declared:

"Mr. George Meredith is a clever man, without literary
genius, taste or judgment. The effect of the book on us is that

of clever, meretricious, turbid pictures by a man of some vigour, jaunty manners, quick observation, and some pictorial skill, who likes writing about naked human passions, but does not bring either original imaginative power or true sentiment to the task." It said further:

"He sometimes treats serious themes with a flippant levity that is exceedingly vulgar and unpleasant." The volume was not received very pleasantly by any publication.

In that summer (1862) Meredith contemplated sharing a house in Chelsea with Swinburne and Dante Gabriel Rossetti. The house was No. 16 Cheyne Walk. Meredith spent a day in London each week in connection with his post as reader for Messrs. Chapman & Hall, and it seemed simpler to spend one night a week in Chelsea than to return late to Copsham Cottage.

The house in Cheyne walk was inhabited by D. G. Rossetti, his brother W. M. Rossetti, Swinburne and Meredith, but W. M. Rossetti and Meredith came and went. They dined in common when they were in residence.

From the beginning of this arrangement, Meredith failed to fit in with the rest. It may have been D. G. Rossetti's artistic atmosphere which irritated him. W. M. Rossetti explained matters thus:

"Mr. Meredith was incomparably more a man of the world and a man of society. . . . Even in the matter of household routine, he found that Rossetti's (D. G.'s) arrangements, though ample for comfort of a more or less off-hand kind, were not comfortable to his standard." Perhaps several poets under one roof are too many, perhaps it was the aristocrat in Meredith coming uppermost. It is alleged that Meredith's departure was hastened by the spectacle of D. G. Rossetti at a late breakfast when he is said to have "devoured like an ogre five poached eggs that had slowly bled to death on five slabs of bacon".

For whatever reason, Meredith's sub-tenancy at 16 Cheyne Walk only lasted about eighteen months.

By now he had an assured income apart from fiction and poetry. Not only did he act as reader for Chapman & Hall, but in 1860 he had become a member of the staff of *The Ipswich Journal*, the leading East Anglian newspaper. He wrote for it leading articles and a kind of London Letter at a salary of about £200 a year. It was in the same year that he became reader for Chapman & Hall, who probably paid him as much. In 1860 an income of £400 a year more than equalled one of £800 a year today. He lived modestly, and beyond his little son had no one dependent on him.

In 1862 also, Arthur Meredith, now nine years old, went to school. His father placed him in the care of the Rev. Augustus Jessopp, headmaster of King Edward VI's School, Norwich. In the beginning of their acquaintance Dr. Jessopp had written to Meredith admiring his work, and a friendship had developed in consequence. The parting from Arthur affected him deeply, and he spent some time at Norwich as Jessopp's guest until he had seen Arthur happily established in his new surroundings. Arthur had begun school in the autumn term, and Meredith, still the indulgent father, planned great festivities for the first Christmas holidays. They stayed with the Hardmans in London and went to the pantomime at Drury Lane on Boxing Day.

Partings seem to have affected Arthur far less than his father, for on his return to school, after a strange feast of oysters and cakes, he said at the railway station:

"Never mind, Papa; it is no use minding it; I shall soon be back to you." Yet Meredith continued to fuss over the calm child more like a doting mother than a reasonable father. They spent the summer holidays of 1863 at Seaford, with a party of Meredith's friends which included Maurice Fitzgerald and Francis Burnand, whom we have met already, and H. M. Hyndman. The last has left a record of what is probably the most sound criticism of Meredith ever made. It came from Francis Burnand, when these friends were idling on the beach while Meredith talked with the astonishing charm which captivated most people who came in contact with him. At last Burnand burst out:

"Damn you, George, why won't you write as you talk?"

If only Meredith had taken this advice he would be more widely read than he is. No excuse can be found for a writer who creates deliberately an obscure, difficult style. In Meredith's case it was probably a form of vanity, though it may have represented a striving after excellence. Swinburne could not abide it, and offended Meredith by admitting that he was quite unable to read *One of Our Conquerors*, *Lord Ormont and his Aminta*, and *The Amazing Marriage*. Swinburne, having read *Beauchamp's Career*, wrote to John Morley:

"What a noble book it might and should have been, if he would but have forgone his lust of epigram and habit of trying to tell a story by means of riddles that hardly excite the curiosity they are certain to baffle!"

For the benefit of those unacquainted with Meredith's style an extract from a parody of it by Sir Max Beerbohm, published in the Christmas number of the *Saturday Review* in 1896, may be quoted. Sir Max's title for the alleged Meredithian novel is "The Victory of Aphasia Ghibberish":

"In the heart of insular Cosmos, remote by some scores of leagues of hodge-trod arable or pastoral—not more than half a snuff-pinch to gaping tourists' nostrils accustomed to inhalation of prairie winds, but enough for perspective—from these marginal sands, trident-scraped, we are to fancy, by a helmeted Dame Abstract, familiarly profiled on discs of current bronze, price of a loaf for humbler maws disdainful of Gallic side-dishes for the titillation of choicer palates, stands Ghibberish Park, a house of some pretensions, mentioned at Runnymede, with the spreading exception of wings given to it in latter times by Daedalean monsters not to be balked of billiards or traps for Terpsichore, and owned for unbroken generations by a healthy line of procreant Ghibberishes, to the undoing of collateral branches eager for the birth of a female."

This is by no means an exaggeration of Meredith's style. In fact, anyone who has struggled with the opening chapters of *One of Our Conquerors* might describe it as an understatement. Those unfamiliar with Meredith are advised to begin with *The Ordeal of Richard Feverel*. There they will find a charming love story which atones for the ridiculous figure of "Sir Austin Absworthy Bearne Feverel, Baronet, of Raynham Abbey, in a certain western county folding Thames", the prig Richard, the laboured epigrams, and the dreadful snobbery which blasts so tremendous a social gulf between Ripton Thompson, son of Sir Austin's solicitor, and Richard, the young Bart-to-be.

Here is Meredith's description of his heroine, Lucy:

"She was indeed sweetly fair, and would have been held fair among rival damsels. . . . The soft rose in her cheeks, the clearness of her eyes, bore witness to the body's virtue; and health and happy blood were in her bearing . . . the wide summer-hat, nodding over her forehead to her brows, seemed to flow with the glowingly heavy curls, and those fire-threaded mellow curls, only half curls, waves of hair call them, rippling at the ends, went like a sunny red-veined torrent down her back almost to her waist; a glorious vision to the youth (Richard) who embraced it as a flower of beauty, and read not a feature.

"There were curious features of colour in her face for him to have read. Her brows, thick and brownish against a soft skin showing the action of the blood, met in the bend of a bow, extending to the temples long and level: you saw that she was fashioned to peruse the sights of earth, and by the pliability of her brows that the wonderful creature used her faculty, and was not going to be a statue to the gazer. Under the dark thick brows an arch of lashes shot out, giving a wealth of darkness to the full frank blue eyes, a mystery of meaning— more than brain was ever meant to fathom."

No really spiritual reader could help falling a little in love with Lucy. Her description is taken from the fifteenth chapter of *The Ordeal of Richard Feverel*, and the man, or woman, who could read that chapter, and not give a sigh for his, or her, lost illusions is fit for treasons, stratagems, and spoils, and may not be trusted.

Robert Louis Stevenson (q.v.) said of Meredith: "He is the Master of us all." A very respectable critic has written of him:

"The idiosyncrasies of his style, which in the later works is often provokingly compressed and elliptical, form a certain barrier to appreciation, and repel many at the outset; but those who have become accustomed to the atmosphere of his thought and utterance are agreed that there are few writers, living or dead, whose works will better repay a careful study. Unintelligence and obscurity are relative terms; and to the novel in its most complete and highest form it cannot be made a matter of reproach that there are some—perhaps many—who lack the intelligence or the sensibility that can alone admit them to the charmed circle of appreciative readers."

To me, simplicity of style is the greatest virtue, and I have always advised young writers to read the first chapter of the Book of Genesis (Authorised Version), where the story of the Creation is told incomparably, in words mostly of one syllable. ("And God said: 'Let there be light,' and there was light") and model their style on that. But every great man is entitled to his particular affectation; as Meredith delighted in a deliberate obscurity of style, his readers must put up with it, or go without Meredith. No one can say whether Meredith would have written better if he had written more simply.

In August 1863 Meredith visited Paris, set out on a walking tour with a friend through Dauphine, crossed into Italy, and continued to Switzerland. Meredith returned to England alone, and worked on his novel *Sandra Belloni*. He looked forward to Arthur's arrival for the Christmas holidays. Yet at this very moment a happening loomed ahead which was to put Arthur's nose for ever out of joint.

In the autumn of 1863 Meredith had met a girl. She was Marie Vulliamy, the youngest of a Mr. Justin Vulliamy's three daughters, and her age was twenty-four. The Vulliamys lived in Mickleham Vale, near Esher. Marie Vulliamy made a great impression on Meredith, but nothing happened immediately.

In April 1864 he stayed with Dr. and Mrs. Jessopp at Norwich, and, strangely enough, Marie Vulliamy was staying in Norwich, too. Amid the well-known delights of Norwich he proposed to her, they returned to London together, and shortly afterwards the engagement was announced. Dr. Jessopp married them at Mickleham Church on September 20th, 1864.

They spent their honeymoon at Southampton and Bursledon, stayed with Marie's father for Christmas, and then at last Meredith was compelled to give up his beloved cottage at the edge of Copsham Common. It could not accommodate his wife, himself, and Arthur in the holidays. Therefore the Merediths lodged for a time at Esher, proceeded from Esher to Kingston-on-Thames, and finally leased Kingston Lodge, Norbiton, opposite Norbiton Hall, home of William ("Tuck") Hardman, Meredith's great friend, whom we have met already.

It is convenient to dispose here of Arthur Meredith, who fades from the picture after his father's marriage.

Ever since the departure of Meredith's first wife, Mary Ellen (it is curious that both his wives had the Christian name of Mary), he had spent all his affection on Arthur. From a remark of Arthur's quoted above, it may be seen that he was a rather spoiled child. His affection for his father did not equal his father's for him. But when a rival appeared on the scene in the shape of a stepmother, all Arthur's possessive instinct rose up, and he became violently jealous. No longer did he rule the home in his holidays, and when a child of the second marriage arrived in 1865, Arthur being then twelve, he could hardly endure the presence of another child in his home.

As he grew older he grew no wiser, nor less jealous. He left Norwich in 1867, and continued his education in Switzerland and Germany. Meredith and he wrote to one another till 1872, and then the correspondence lapsed. Eventually Arthur began a business career in France. He became ill, and in 1881 Meredith invited him to come and live at Box Hill, which was then Meredith's home. Arthur refused the invitation, and convalesced on the Continent. He did not regain his health, and in 1889 took a voyage to Australia. The other passenger in his cabin was a hopeless drunkard, which did not contribute to Arthur's happiness.

His health improved at Sydney, but he only survived his return to England a few months, and died at Woking on September 3rd, 1890.

Meredith now entered on a highly productive period. In 1864 *Emilia in England*, afterwards known as *Sandra Belloni* appeared, and *Rhoda Fleming* and *Vittoria* in 1865 and 1866. He had some trouble with *Emilia* (or *Sandra*), but he was breaking away from his usual style, and attempting the novel of character. The tailoring *motif* appears again, as in *Evan Harrington*, but this time three sisters are involved. The shame of tailoring as an occupation must have impressed him very deeply to make two novels hinging on the abhorred shears seem worth while to him. Surrey provides some of the background for the novel.

Emilia received praise from the reviewers, but *Rhoda Fleming* did not sell well, and brought no kindly reviews. With the exception of *Richard Feverel*, it is my favourite among his novels, and I have not been influenced by R. L. Stevenson's comment that the novel is the strongest thing in English letters since Shakespeare died, partly because I read the book before reading Stevenson's comment, partly because the book is nothing of the kind. Stevenson allowed his admiration for Meredith to run away with his judgment. Scenes from Surrey appear in this novel also.

By now Meredith's financial worries had ceased. Chapman & Hall increased his salary; he continued his journalism; and the return brought by his novels mounted. I think that from this point he really began to live. The fatal mistake of his early marriage had ended, his feverish obsession with Arthur was over, and he had entered happily on a second, successful marriage. The obsession with Arthur probably represented a sacrifice of atonement. In some undefined way he wished to excuse to Arthur the lack of a mother, and to himself the want of success of his first marriage. The failure of that marriage must have dealt a fatal blow to his self-pride. Now Marie Vulliamy had blotted out its memory, and he could square his shoulders and hold his head high.

Vittoria forms a sequel to *Emilia in England* (*Sandra Belloni*), and deals with the Italian rising of 1848. In June 1866 Meredith acted as war correspondent for the *Morning Post* in the war between Italy and Austria. He was not a good war correspondent, as those familiar with his style may imagine, but, thanks to his campaign with the Italian Army, he was able to add touches to *Vittoria*, which had appeared originally as a serial in the *Fortnightly Review*, before Chapman & Hall published the novel early in 1867.

Nobody seems to have cared greatly for *Vittoria* at the time of publication, except Swinburne, who loved Italy, and Meredith despaired a little. But the end of 1867 was happy, because it was then that he moved to Flint Cottage, Box Hill, his home for the rest of his life.

The cottage, which still exists, stands at the foot of Box Hill. Just as Dickens erected a chalet in the gardens of Gad's Hill in which to work, so, about ten years after he took Flint Cottage, Meredith built a working chalet at the highest part of his garden, with a sleeping room opening out of the room in which he worked. Flint Cottage was his first and only real home; here his daughter, Marie Eveleen, was born in 1871, and here he did his most important work.

At the beginning of his tenancy he worked on *The Adventures of Harry Richmond*. It was serialised in the *Cornhill Magazine* and ran for fifteen months, the novel being published by Smith, Elder, late in 1871. It is a novel of gypsy life, and is superior to the work of George Borrow, in the opinion of Theodore Watts-Dunton. The story is autobiographical, in the sense that *David Copperfield* is autobiographical, and scenes from the life of Meredith and his family are recognisable. Like *Evan Harrington*, it is something of a snob novel.

Opinions about it differed; thus, Arthur Symonds wrote that "On a first reading we are fairly swept away and carried along by the racing tide of the narrative"; W. L. Courtney, on the other hand, wrote:

"Perhaps in no novel do we find the absence of joy more conspicuous than in *Harry Richmond* . . . he is never young, but talks about himself with a *maladie de la pensée* of a modern age." Evidently it is impossible for even a Meredith to please everyone; the absence of joy may be related to Meredith's own youth and its joyless nature. Probably in his adolescence he, too, talked about himself with a *maladie de la pensée*.

The instructed few admired the novel, but the world at large was not impressed.

There followed *Beauchamp's Career*, completed in 1874, serialised in the *Fortnightly Review*, and published by Chapman & Hall in 1875. Here again Meredith achieved no general appeal. Beauchamp himself is derivative, his character being based on that of Meredith's friend, Captain Frederick Maxse, R.N. He suffers from an internal conflict between his own aristocratic ideas and a sympathy with what it is fashionable nowadays to refer to as "the Common Man."

In the succeeding few years he completed no large piece of work, but in 1877 the chalet in the garden had been constructed, and here he wrote *The Egoist*, generally considered the most brilliant of his novels. He did not finish it until the beginning of 1879, and it has a tragic significance, because overwork while completing it permanently affected his health. Kegan, Paul & Co., published it in 1879.

Publication of *The Egoist* marked the turn of the tide. From then onward his fame rested secure. The leading reviews praised the novel unstintedly, and the faithful R. L. Stevenson and W. E. Henley became reciprocally lyrical. It has moved one of Meredith's biographers to an almost Meredithian piece of prose:

"Certainly *The Egoist* must be immortal, for despite its cold glittering artificiality and intellectual and philosophical preciosity, the sheer cleverness of the book, its wealth of epigram, the concatenation of antithesis and antiperistasis (Antiperistasis: accent on the second I: 'Opposition or contrast of circumstances.'), make it unique, a towering Alpine peak in literature, crested with eternal gleaming snows."

The plot of *The Egoist* is simple. A critic has defined the novel as "a study of the most refined form of self-preoccupation, presented through a marvellously searching analysis of the subtleties of motive, accompanied by a free play of genial satire". The egoist of the novel is Sir Willoughby Patterne, in whom all its readers can see themselves mirrored. Meredith himself declared of Sir Willoughby:

"He is all of us." This may explain the fact that *The Egoist* made a more universal appeal than its forerunners.

The rest of Meredith's novels are *The Tragic Comedians* (1881), *Diana of the Crossways* (1885), *One of Our Conquerors* (1891), *Lord Ormont and His Aminta* (1894) and *The Amazing Marriage* (1895). There were also three small volumes of verse, *Poems and Lyrics of the Joy of Earth* (1883), *Ballads and Poems of Tragic Life* (1887) and *A Reading of Earth* (1888).

The Egoist marked a turning point in more ways than one. It coincided with a change in Meredith's style. He could now write as he liked, for his finances made him independent of public approval, and in consequence there arrived a tendency to "show them"; to demonstrate that if his style had chastised many with whips in the past, he was capable of chastening them with scorpions.

"There was a marked change," writes one commentator, "in Mr. Meredith's style, a change not without its disadvantages—to a more fastidious choice of words, with an increasing command of felicitous phrases, and a more sedulous effort to put the fullest significance and suggestiveness into every sentence."

Those who will study the opening chapters of *Diana of the Crossways* and *One of Our Conquerors* will appreciate the result.

Of these novels, *Diana of the Crossways* has the most interesting associations. The prototype of Diana was Mrs. Norton, one of the three beautiful Sheridan sisters, the others being Mrs. Blackwood and Lady Seymour. Caroline Norton had black hair, coiled round her head, and an adorable trick of blushing. Her features resembled those of a Greek goddess. All three were grand-daughters of Richard Brinsley Sheridan.

Mrs. Norton made an unsuccessful marriage with George Norton, a younger brother of the third Lord Grantley. In 1836, being then in her twenty-eighth year (she married at the age of twenty), she was involved with the Prime Minister, Lord Melbourne, in divorce proceedings begun by her husband, whose case failed. In 1845 she was supposed to have sold to *The Times*, then edited by Delane, the secret of the imminent repeal of the Corn Laws. This accusation was false.

Meredith repeated the accusation in *Diana of the Crossways*, but after 1896 added a note to the effect that Mrs. Norton had been proved innocent of the charge. He met her, when she had reached the age of fifty, at the Duff Gordons' House, but she had been dead four years when he began to write *Diana of the Crossways*.

W. E. Henley, in the *Athenaeum*, declared that Meredith approached Shakespeare, and that Diana equalled Rosalind. Thus he fell into the same ecstatic exaggeration as his co-admirer of Meredith, R. L. Stevenson.

Meredith's working life ended in 1895 with his novel *The Amazing Marriage*, though he lived till 1909. It remains to consider the man himself.

He was proud, haughty, and super-sensitive, with a good deal of vanity in his make-up. This vanity led him to believe, even to the end of his days, when he had become world-famous as a writer, that reviewers never did him justice. As we have seen, this contention was groundless, at any rate after the publication of *The Egoist*.

He cannot have been an easy man for a woman to live with, and the happiness and success of his second marriage probably resulted from the fact that the second Mrs. Meredith was half French. French women understand men better than English women, and are more practical and less "romantic" about men than their English sisters.

She was tactful, considerate, and good-looking, interesting to talk to, and a musician. Knowing herself married to a genius, she took the greatest care of him, a necessary precaution because all his life he suffered from digestive troubles, probably of nervous origin. But he loved good food and good wine, although at one time he insisted on becoming a vegetarian. Mrs. Meredith, who saw him grow thinner, and more irritable, and knew that a man who worked hard and took much exercise required nourishment, said nothing, but persuaded the local baker to mix minced meat with Meredith's bread. She died in 1885, after an operation.

So, in his last ten years, Meredith gradually declined into a literary legend, and became that rather grim figure, a Sage; the Sage of Box Hill. The University of St. Andrews conferred the degree of LL.D. on him in 1892. In that year his son, William Maxse, married, and two years later his daughter, Marie Eveleen, married also. She went to live at Leatherhead, not far from her father.

By this time he had become very deaf, and spoke in a loud voice. He suffered from Dr. Johnson's weakness for monopolising the conversation, and it was not considered good form to contradict him, particularly as he disliked contradiction. He became the arbiter of his circle. In 1898, on the occasion of his seventieth birthday, he received an address signed by among others, J. M. Barrie, Thomas Hardy, Henry James, and Swinburne. In 1903 he suffered a severe illness, and almost died. King Edward VII gave him the Order of Merit in 1905, though he was too much of an invalid to receive the Order from his Sovereign at Buckingham Palace.

At that period the picture of him is that of an invalid, for in the autumn of 1905 he broke a leg, and subsequently could only move in a bath-chair. This vehicle was drawn by a donkey named "Picnic", and beside it walked Miss Nicholls, his nurse-attendant. On his eightieth birthday, in 1908, two hundred and fifty distinguished people signed a congratulatory address. He received also an address from the Society of Authors, of which he was president, and gave an audience to the Press. The *Daily Telegraph's* representative wrote:

"A wonderful old man, with a face like Hermes grown old, the long white hair lying loosely about his ears, with a rug round his knees and his hand to his ear. . . . When he spoke, the deep, rich, resonant voice, and the animation of the countenance, seemed to give added stature to the aged frame. . . . Mr. Meredith was characteristically modest. 'I have been climbing the stairs for eighty years,' he exclaimed, 'and I have done with the pulpit.'"

He lived to see his eighty-first birthday, February 12th, 1909. On May 14th he caught a chill, and died four days later. He sleeps beside his second wife in Dorking cemetery.

Meredith was a great man, and a great writer. If his style is often difficult, the reader should learn to appreciate it for the sake of his own soul, and Meredith's many virtues. One has to learn to appreciate art, and the same necessity applies to literature. As Trollope said of Dickens, no young writer should try to imitate Meredith, for the young writer will only copy the mannerisms, and be incapable of reproducing the matter.

Meredith's judgment as a publisher's reader was typical of himself. He might well have ruined his firm, for he only praised what appealed to his exclusive taste, in spite of the fact that publishers are in business to make profits, and need books that will sell in quantity. Thus, Meredith refused the work of *Ouida*, Mrs. Henry Wood, and Mrs. Lynn Linton, and Samuel Butler's *Erewhon*. On the other hand, he encouraged the young Thomas Hardy.

It is an interesting comment on the times in which we live to reflect that if Meredith were a young author today he could not have afforded to write purely to please himself and never for the pot. Taxation in his time was negligible, and so, with a small income, he was able to live, as a young married man with a child, in sufficient comfort to enable him to produce the best that was in him.

We may well let Oscar Wilde deliver the final verdict on Meredith, since, for all his studied flippancies and affectations, Wilde had impeccable taste where writing was concerned. He wrote in 1891:

"One incomparable novelist we have now in England, Mr. George Meredith. There are better artists in France, but France has no one whose view of life is so large, so varied, so imaginatively true. . . .

"To him belongs philosophy in fiction. His people not merely live, but they live in thought. One can see them from a myriad points of view. . . . And he who made them, those wonderful quickly moving figures, made them for his own pleasure, and has never asked the public what they wanted, has never cared to know what they wanted, has never allowed the public to dictate to him or influence him in any way, but has gone on intensifying his own personality, and producing his own individual work. At first none came to him. That did not matter. Then the few came to him. That did not change him. The many have come now. He is still the same. He is an incomparable novelist."

ROBERT LOUIS STEVENSON
(1850–1894)

ROBERT LOUIS STEVENSON

From the canvas (unfinished) by Sir William Blake Richmond
now in the National Portrait Gallery

ROBERT LOUIS STEVENSON
(1850–1894)

IN SOME respects one finds it difficult to be patient with
Stevenson. The naïve egoism of his letters becomes
wearisome; the calm negligence with which he depended
on his father for his upkeep, his idleness at school and Edinburgh
University, and the rather helpless way in which he took all
his troubles to various women, grate on the normal man. In
his favour it must be said that he was always an invalid, and
that he had the characteristic optimism of those whom doctors
term "thoracic cases".

From his earliest days he was a spoiled child, doted on by
his parents and his nurse, Alison Cunningham, whom he
nicknamed "Cummy", to whom he dedicated *A Child's Garden
of Verses*. His mother recorded his infant pronouncements, and
his father lingered outside his bedroom door at night and logged
his childish babble in a notebook. How Thomas Stevenson,
the father, a tough Scots engineer, descended from a line of
engineers, managed to become a complaisant worshipper of
his own extension in the person of his small son, is a psychological mystery difficult to explain. Even the doting Thomas
was to show a certain impatience with him before Thomas
passed on to a better land.

Robert Louis Stevenson could trace his pedigree back to
the fifteenth century on his mother's side and the seventeenth
on his father's. His mother was Margaret Balfour, of the Balfours of Pilrig, and he was christened Robert Lewis Balfour.
Up to his sixteenth year he signed himself "R. Stevenson",
and then, in a moment of adolescent expansion, asked his
mother to call him "Robert Louis" and signed himself "R. L.
Stevenson" until the year 1873. At the age of eighteen he
altered the spelling of "Lewis" to "Louis", thus annoying the
Balfours; Lewis was his Balfour grandfather's name, and the
name of several Balfour cousins, called after the grandfather.

All this represented an early sign of a certain showiness which distinguished him, another symptom of which was the famous velveteen jacket of later years.

He was born on November 13th, 1850, at No. 8 Howard Place, Edinburgh; his mother noted in her diary that he had eyes "blue at first, turning to hazel" and that his hair was "very fair—almost none at first".

The first-born usually resembles the parent of opposite sex, and this was true of Stevenson. Unfortunately, not only did his face resemble hers, but he inherited her delicate constitution and tendency to chest troubles. Yet Mrs. Stevenson could hardly have been so delicate as she was made' out to be. She survived her husband and her son, and in 1891, a widow, aged sixty-two, left Scotland to live with Stevenson and his wife in Samoa.

Three months before Stevenson's birth, his famous grandfather, designer of lighthouses, who built the Bell Rock Lighthouse, died and his son, Thomas, Stevenson's father, carried on the family tradition of lighthouse building, intending, in due time, to hand down the tradition to his son, Robert Louis. In this Thomas Stevenson was to be disappointed, but he seems to have met the disappointment without a word of complaint.

I cannot help finding Thomas Stevenson more of a hero than his more famous son. He had a better face for one thing, with a fine massive forehead, keen, steady eyes, a strong chin with a cleft in it, and a firm, level mouth which contradicted his kindly nature. Nor did he wear a velveteen jacket, but a morning coat, as befitted a man of standing in Edinburgh and Scotland. He was also, like his father before him, Engineer to the Board of Northern Lights, as grand a title as ever a man had, with the care of the twenty lighthouses his father had built along the coasts of Scotland.

Stevenson was born in the first year of his parents' marriage. A girl friend and bridesmaid of his mother's described him, during a visit to his parents in 1851, as "a fractious little fellow, though decidedly pretty with his dark eyes and fair hair. This uncommon combination he inherited from his mother, from her also his light heart, which carried him bravely through the many years of delicacy that would have depressed most people into thorough invalidism".

Until he became fifteen he was known in the family by the pet name of "Smout". Since the Scots refer to a cow as a "coo" (compare "Auld Robin Gray", by Lady Anne Barnard:

> "*He hadna been gone a twelvemonth and a day*
> *When my father brake his arm and the coo was stown away*")

probably "Smout" was pronounced "Smoot".

By January 1853 the Thomas Stevensons had moved to No. 1 Inverleith Terrace. They took it from Professor and Mrs. Aytoun, he being that William Edmonstoune Aytoun, Professor of English Literature at Edinburgh University, who wrote *Lays of the Cavaliers*, which, to adapt a phrase from Mr. Jorrocks, are the image of Scott with twenty-five per cent of his genius.

Thomas Stevenson, in view of his wife's and his baby's tendency to diseases of the chest, showed rather reprehensible carelessness in taking this house. Professor Aytoun gave it up because of its dampness. He told a friend that a white silk dress "which recalls indistinct reminiscences of the altar" hung in a bag there. The Professor continued:

"Blight and mildew! It was spotted like a leopard's skin."

In addition to being damp, the house faced north, and in Edinburgh at that.

No. 1 Inverleith Terrace started Stevenson on his long, long trail of illnesses. He had a bad attack of croup there, and afterwards went down with some complaint or other every year. From this house he first went to school, being teased a great deal because of his strange appearance.

In his sixth year he first became an author. An uncle had offered a prize (a Bible picture book) for the best history of Moses, to be competed for by his children and his nephews. Stevenson won it; he could print letters and draw, but he could not read. Consequently his mother took down the letterpress from dictation and he did the coloured illustrations himself. The Israelites are shown going out of Egypt in trousers and tall hats, and Moses is smoking a pipe.

Probably thousands of little boys have done something of the kind and remained obscure. However, Stevenson and his mother took this history of Moses seriously; he said that he wanted to be an author, and she believed him capable of fulfilling his ambition.

Finally a doctor, called in on account of the child's bronchitis, said that the house was too cold for him and so, in May 1857, the family moved once more, to 17 Heriot Row, a sunny place looking into lawns and gardens. There the Stevensons remained for life.

The parents were deeply religious, and the child passed his early life in a Calvinistic atmosphere. His nurse, just as religious as his parents, taught him the shorter Catechism and read the Bible to him. He was brought up on such books as *The Scottish Worthies* and *Fox's Book of Martyrs*. Sunday was a grim day for the small Stevenson.

Some of his happiest memories of childhood centred on the Manse of his grandfather, the Rev. Lewis Balfour, at Colinton, over which his aunt, Jane Whyte Balfour, presided. The Manse stood beside a river, always a romantic situation for a child, and there was a wonderful garden. The young Stevenson used to put his ear against the graveyard wall so that the spirits of the dead could speak to him, and watched from the windows of the Manse after dark hoping to see ghosts gibbering among the graves.

At the age of seven he continued his very spasmodic education, interrupted as it was by frequent illnesses, at a school kept by a Mr. Henderson. He only stayed a few weeks, for illness claimed him almost at once. He returned there in 1859 and remained until 1861, when he began at the famous Edinburgh Academy.

There must have been something queer about him as a child, for here, as at his first school, the other boys ragged him; though it is true that a boy more intelligent than the rest is always ragged at school, since mediocrity cannot endure intelligence. School did not trouble him a great deal, for his parents travelled frequently and took him with them, and Thomas Stevenson did not view his son's school career very seriously. In 1863, for instance, we find him at Mentone for two months because of Mrs. Stevenson's health; continuing thence to Genoa, Naples, Rome, Florence, and Venice, and coming home by way of the Rhine. Probably Stevenson learned a great deal more during this holiday than he would have learned at any school, even Edinburgh Academy.

He did not return there. He went to his aunt, Jane Balfour, who now lived near London, her father being dead, because the doctor sent his mother once more to Mentone. He became a boarder for a term at a school at Spring Grove, and hated it as the unusual boy always hates school, for which he is too old mentally. He wrote to his father on the eve of his thirteenth birthday begging to be taken away, and Thomas Stevenson transported him to Mentone in time for Christmas.

His parents made another attempt to educate him on their return to Edinburgh, and on and off, from 1864 to 1867, he studied at one of those unmentionable establishments, a private school for backward or delicate boys, in Frederick Street, Edinburgh.

It seems odd that Thomas Stevenson should have considered this spasmodic and haphazard education suitable for a future Engineer to the Board of Northern Lights, for that was what he intended his son to become.

Stevenson was now (1867) seventeen; a tall youth, rather narrow in the shoulders, with fair hair, an insatiable curiosity about everything, and a passion for discussing anything and everything. All his life he was to be remembered for the art of conversation; with him, as with other passionate conversationalists less famous, it was difficult for anyone else to get a word in edgeways. Like a thousand other boys, he collected birds' eggs and wild flowers; he learned French at Mentone and German at Torquay. He rambled about Scotland, and in the course of his rambling arrived at Peebles where he was taught by the Master of the Burgh School, who declared him the most intelligent and best-informed boy he had ever known.

"The boy," writes a biographer, "grew up precocious, interesting, affected, and egregiously egotistic." He was the only child of doting parents, and little else could have been expected.

At the age of fifteen he wrote his first novel. It was called: *The Pentland Rising: A Page of History, 1666*, and fond Thomas Stevenson paid for its publication in the form of a pamphlet, price 4d., of which one hundred copies were printed. Fond Mrs. Stevenson bought most of the copies. Today *The Pentland Rising* is a collector's piece.

In May 1867, Mr. and Mrs. Stevenson took Swanston Cottage, in a valley of the Pentland Hills, and there they passed spring and summer. There seems, for Stevenson, to have been some magic in this place. He loved it from the beginning, and throughout life. The milder climate of the sheltered valley improved his health, and he could always have a friend to stay there if he chose. Since the invincible charm which distinguished his entire life had already come upon him, he made friends of all the village. It is all described minutely in his unfinished novel, *St. Ives*.

November of each year put an end to the family summering at Swanston Cottage, and in November 1867 Stevenson was enrolled at Edinburgh University, and put himself down for classes in Latin and Greek, neither of which he ever attended. Indeed, though he passed seven sessions at the University he did no work whatever. He has described himself at the University thus:

"A certain lean, ugly, idle, unpopular student, whose presence was for me the gist and heart of the whole matter, whose changing humours, fine occasional purposes of good, flinching acceptance of evil, shiverings on wet, east-windy morning journeys up to class, infinite yawnings during lectures, and unquenchable gusto in the delights of truantry, made up the sunshine and shadow of my college life."

The explanation of his unpopularity is peculiar. As he did no work, he could hardly make friends among those who worked, but there was another reason. As J. W. Mackail puts it:

"Even as a boy, he was completely wrapped up in two interests: literature, and the curious study of human life in all its respects, with a strong leaning towards its more sordid and squalid aspects, and as strong a revolt against convention and respectability."

The average Scottish University student is a worker, and looks on his University career as the greatest opportunity in his life. He does not mean to waste this opportunity through idleness. Stevenson, the only child of wealthy parents, did not care whether he worked or not, and chose not to work. Therefore the other students formed a poor opinion of him as an idler, but there was more: they did not care for his friends and the society, apart from his parent's friends, in which he mixed. It was not the type of society with which hard-working young men with their way to make could afford to associate. It had too many "sordid and squalid aspects".

Thomas Stevenson, still nursing the unconquerable hope, still clutching the inviolable shade, continued to believe that his son would become an engineer. As Stevenson had not specialised in mathematics, the illusion seems remarkable. In 1868 his father sent him to Anstruther, where harbour works were in progress, that he might learn from observation. He hated engineering, and wrote to his mother that he wanted to go back to Swanston. Instead he was directed to Wick, to observe more engineering work, where he made a practice dive in diving dress.

After these samples of the family profession he returned to Edinburgh, and put himself down, in the University session of 1868, for the Latin class only, forsaking Greek. Apparently he found it easier to stay away from one class than from two. A more congenial happening occurred in March 1869, when he became a member of the Speculative Society, a very dignified association with a long roll of distinguished members from Sir Walter Scott downwards. That summer his persevering father took him on a voyage in the *Pharos*, a steamer belonging to the Northern Lights Commissioner, which touched at Orkney and Scotland and Fair Isle. There followed his third season at the University with the usual unsatisfactory results. Apart from neglecting classes, he spoke at a debate at the Speculative Society, and also read a paper.

In 1870 he joined the engineering class; this meant journeys to see practical engineering, and these he enjoyed. Some of the topographical details appeared years afterwards in *Kidnapped*. On one of these journeys he met by chance Sir Edmund Gosse, later to become his friend.

At this period of his life he was going through a curious phase. He had reached the age of twenty, and delighted to find his friends and acquaintances in what can only be called the underworld of Edinburgh. He said himself that his acquaintance was "of what would be called a very low order"; it included seamen, chimney sweeps and thieves, and periodically a face would be missing from the company through the intervention of the police. He confesses that he enjoyed it all, that he was petted and respected, the women were gentle and kind to him, and he was known by the name of "Velvet Coat" from his habit of wearing such a garment.

His parents do not seem to have interfered with these strange goings on beyond limiting his allowance to a pound a month. Thus his popularity with the thieves and chimney sweeps must have depended on personal charm; their love could not possibly have been cupboard love. For the rest, he could share all the advantages of home life, but on the question of money his father remained adamant. Perhaps he realised that money meant nothing to his son, who usually got rid of his allowance within twenty-four hours of receiving it.

To the credit side of this kind of life may be put down the fact that wherever he went he made notes. In his own heart he was already a writer, in spite of the Board of Northern Lights. Also he was a born *poseur*, and probably took an adolescent delight in plumbing such sinks of iniquity as the Edinburgh of his day provided. He could not have come to much harm in them on a pound a month, for if the wages of sin is death, the cost of sin has always come high. Unlike Joseph in the Old Testament, one does not go down into the pit for nothing.

Through all his vague and wandering interests the writing interest remained constant. It received a certain stimulus during the winter of 1870. In November of that year three senior students proposed to found a University magazine, and to Stevenson's delight—they were all four members of the Speculative Society—asked him to join them. The *Edinburgh University Magazine* had a brief existence of four months; Stevenson contributed to it six times, and these contributions are preserved in his collected writings.

In March 1871 he read a paper before the Royal Scottish Academy of Arts entitled "A New Form of Intermittent Light for Lighthouses", for which the Society of Arts awarded him a medal. Poor Thomas Stevenson's heart must have fluttered. Perhaps, after all, his wayward and wandering sheep, who was still staying away from Professor Fleeming Jenkin's classes in Mathematics, Natural Philosophy, Engineering, and Mechanical Drawing had the stuff of an Engineer to the Board of Northern Lights in him after all.

Thomas Stevenson found himself illuminated on this point on the 8th day of the following month. On that day Stevenson took his father for a walk, though in the modern idiom he took him for a ride, and explained with adolescent callousness that he could not face the prospect of being an engineer and wanted to make literature his profession.

What this news meant to Thomas Stevenson can be imagined. The family engineering dynasty would expire, and the Engineer to the Board of Northern Lights would no longer be a Stevenson. All he knew of his son was that Robert Louis had idled his way through School and the University, and Thomas Stevenson could understand, for he was a practical man, that no distinguished writer had ever borne the reputation of being an idler. Besides, Robert Louis, at the age of twenty-one, had written nothing to justify a literary career.

It took a lot to shake Thomas Stevenson, who had been contending with rugged nature all his life. As his son testified, he "met the request with calm". He also made a stipulation: since literature was not a recognised profession, as he understood the word "profession", he required his son to read for the Bar. It would do a literary man no harm to become an advocate; also, as Thomas Stevenson may have reflected rather wanly, the calling of an advocate is respectable, and confers a certain social *cachet*. An advocate, obviously, cannot consort with seamen, chimney sweeps, and thieves, not in Edinburgh at any rate, or "scrape acquaintance with all classes of man and womankind", as Stevenson confessed to doing in his student days.

Relieved at his release from engineering, he agreed to read for the Bar, and in October 1871 he began Law classes at the University. The dullness of these was lightened by the arrival of his cousin and life-long associate. R. A. M. Stevenson came to live near Edinburgh, and the two joined forces. Louis was ill that winter, and took a holiday in March 1872, when the air of Dunblane seems to have restored him. Two months later he began to study conveyancing in the office of a Writer to the Signet, and found it a tedious occupation. Amateur theatricals at the house of Professor Fleeming Jenkin relieved his boredom, for if he had stayed away from the Professor's lectures he enjoyed his friendship and that of his wife. Besides, he did not work very hard in the office of Messrs. Skene, Edwards & Bilton, any more than Disraeli did in the office of Messrs. Swain, Steven, Maples, Pearse & Hunt. Stevenson had not the slightest ambition to become an advocate.

After two months of conveyancing he went on holiday to Brussels and Frankfort with Sir Walter Simpson, whose father invented chloroform, who has found immortality by making a canoe journey from Antwerp to Pontoise in company with his friend in 1876. This resulted in Stevenson's first published work *An Inland Voyage*, which appeared in 1878.

But for the moment we are still in the year 1872. Returning from his holiday, Stevenson renewed, in October, his struggles with the University. That winter produced quarrels with his father, and the only marvel is that they had not taken place sooner. Like so many wars, they broke out over the subject of religion. Stevenson had concluded that he could no longer believe the religion in which he had been brought up. Thomas Stevenson believed implicitly in the letter of the Shorter Catechism.

There was more to it than that, and the religious differences merely set alight his anger at his son's goings on in general. Now, apparently, he was an atheist. No wonder he behaved as he did, and consorted with the rabble of Edinburgh.

This quarrel took place in January 1873, but in the following May something happened which restored Thomas Stevenson's opinion of his son. On the evening of May 19th Stevenson read a paper "On the Thermal Influence of Forests" to the Royal Society of Edinburgh, of which his father was a member.

Having followed his career so far, we must do him the justice of recognising his natural charm, the artless charm of a child, for to his dying day he exhibited the characteristics of a glorified Rover Scout. As J. W. Mackail wrote of him, "he was one of those persons who in a sense never out-grow their boyhood," and again:

"Even the philosophy of life developed in both his essays and his romances is that rather of a gifted boy than of a mature man. Like his style, it was fully developed in him by the age of five and twenty, and it underwent no change thereafter except, in his last years, an imperceptible and silent reversion towards the traditions of his birth and blood."

The results of this artless charm were important in July 1873, when he visited one of his girl cousins in the deep south, who had married the Rev. Professor Churchill Babington, Disney Professor of Archaeology at Cambridge, who lived at Cockfield Rectory, in Suffolk. He arrived there on foot from Bury St. Edmunds.

What did he wear? (as women always ask concerning another woman). He wore a velvet jacket, a straw hat, and a knapsack on his back. This strange apparition revealed himself to his girl cousin and a friend of hers, a Mrs. Sitwell. He began to talk, and his conversation so shattered Mrs. Sitwell that she wrote to a Mr. (later Sir) Sidney Colvin, a fellow at Trinity College, Cambridge, who was coming to stay at the Rectory, telling him to leave Cambridge at once because they were entertaining an angel unawares in Stevenson.

Mr. Colvin obeyed, and the radiant young man in the black velvet jacket so impressed him that a life-long friendship began. On the face of it this seems strange, because Stevenson had no academic history with which to impress a Fellow of Trinity, and Colvin was academic to the core, for he became Slade Professor of Fine Arts at Cambridge, and Keeper of Prints and Drawings at the British Museum. As a result of this chance meeting he was, eventually, to edit Stevenson's letters and the Edinburgh edition of his works.

There was not only Sidney Colvin, there was Mrs. Sitwell. Colvin recorded that Stevenson "clung to her devotedly for the next two years as to an inspirer, consoler and guide". She became to him what Mrs. Austen had become to the young Disraeli. Colvin also encouraged him, and Colvin could give him the solid counsel of a recognised critic. Equally important, he was no more than five years older than Stevenson, so that they made friends easily.

The visit to Suffolk had become of first importance in Stevenson's life. He went home to Scotland with, for the first time in his history, a definite literary plan. Colvin had told him to go on reading for the Bar—probably Colvin realised that his new friend required a steadying influence—and to write a few essays suitable for publication. In the meantime Stevenson poured out his whole heart in letters to Mrs. Sitwell. He told her of continued disputes with his father. Of course, he should have left home long since, but he remained economically dependent on his father, with no money but his pound a month.

Finally he fell ill, and being advised by no less a person than the Lord Advocate to read for the English Bar, went south again.

In London his illness so increased that he consulted Sir Andrew Clark, the leading physician of the period, and Sir Andrew did not mince matters. Stevenson was to go to the South of France alone. Like all good doctors, Sir Andrew diagnosed the psychological state of his patient, and realised that family conflict had much to do with his physical condition.

We have now reached a turning point in Stevenson's life, and must glance as quickly as possible over the period which intervened before a second turning point, his meeting with the woman whom, later, he married.

At Mentone he was very ill, and wrote complainingly to Mrs. Sitwell:

"My soul is rarely with me here . . . I am a man of seventy. O Medea, kill me or make me young again!" In time he recovered, and saw a violet, and wrote:

"I feel as if my heart were a little bunch of violets in my bosom," which must have been a peculiar feeling, as one realises if one tries to imagine a little bunch of violets in place of one's heart. Presumably the violet-hearted would die from low blood pressure, violets having no energising properties for the propulsion of liquid.

In November (1873) his first published work appeared in the *Portfolio*. It was an essay entitled "On Roads", a not very fruitful subject. Much later, G. K. Chesterton said the last word on roads when he declared:

> "*Before the Roman came to Rye or out to Severn strode,*
> *The rolling English drunkard made the rolling English road.*
> *A reeling road, a rolling road, that rambles round the shire,*
> *And after him the parson ran, the sexton and the squire;*
> *A merry road, a mazy road, and such as we did tread*
> *The night we went to Birmingham by way of Beachy Head.*"

Stevenson, of course, took his essays very seriously. Thomas Stevenson was paying for the holiday at Mentone.

Colvin stayed with him for about three months, and Andrew Lang came to call on Colvin, and so met Stevenson. Lang said Stevenson, who wore his hair long, looked girlish, and Stevenson said Lang was good-looking and Oxfordish. In spite of these opinions they became friends for life.

Stevenson, having finished off the "Roads", had been working on *Ordered South*, and through the recommendation of Colvin, *Macmillian's Magazine* accepted it. In April 1874, he returned to Edinburgh via Paris, where his cousin, R. A. M. Stevenson, the artist already mentioned, lived in a studio. "Bob" introduced Robert Louis to the artistic life of the Latin Quarter.

When he reached Edinburgh a wonderful thing happened. Thomas Stevenson increased his allowance from 5s. a week to £84 a year. Perhaps he did not find himself much better off, as out of his £84 he was to pay for everything except food and lodging, but, having published two essays, he hoped to make more money by writing.

His hopes materialised, for *Cornhill* took an article on Victor Hugo, and *The Fortnightly Review* commissioned a review of Lord Lytton's *Fables in Song*.

In June of that year (1874) the Savile Club elected him a member, and he had to ask his father for the ten guineas subscription. Being now a member of a London club, obviously he must visit London and make his *début* as a clubman. He did, and no doubt Thomas Stevenson paid; and there he became blooded to the contemporary bright young men of literature.

That summer he wrote his articles on "John Knox and His Relations with Women", which may be read in the volume of essays entitled, *Familiar Studies of Men and Books*, but were published originally in *Macmillian's Magazine*. In October, instead of continuing the study of Law in Edinburgh, he departed to England, walked in the Chilterns, and called on Colvin and Mrs. Sitwell in London. Presumably Thomas Stevenson paid once more. The expenses could hardly have come from his £84 a year.

Returning to Edinburgh in November, he faced the dreadful

law classes, and also some work in the office of Messrs. Skene, Edwards & Bilton. In February 1875 there came another important meeting.

Leslie Stephen, then editor of *Cornhill*, journeyed to Edinburgh to see a contributor, whom he described to his wife as "a miserable cripple in the infirmary, who has lost one foot and is likely to lose another—or rather hopes just to save it". He went on to tell her that he was introducing Stevenson to the patient, who was W. E. Henley.

> (*"Out of the night that covers me*
> *Black as the Pit from pole to pole,*
> *I thank whatever gods there be*
> *For my unconquerable soul.*
>
> *In the fell clutch of circumstance*
> *I have not winced, nor cried aloud;*
> *Beneath the bludgeonings of chance*
> *My head is bloody, but unbowed."*)

Thus began another life-long friendship, with Henley, poet and critic.

After the exhaustion of the University session, in April Stevenson departed to Paris and his cousin, R. A. M. Stevenson. The cousin took him to Barbizon—jewelled name—which, though he did not know it, was charged with fate. Back in Edinburgh, he met a man also charged with his fate, one J. Seed, once Secretary to the Customs and Marine Department of New Zealand, who talked of the South Seas, "till" as Stevenson told Mrs. Sitwell in one of his emetic letters, for to this good lady he regurgitated the overplus of his soul's food, "I was sick with desire to go there." The desire remained until fulfilled, and when fulfilled he found fulfilment satisfying, as so seldom happens with fulfilled desires.

An exceedingly strange thing took place in July 1875. In spite of idling at his classes and in the office of Messrs. Skene, Edwards & Bilton, and absences on holiday or through illness from his classes, Stevenson passed his final examination for admission to the Faculty of Advocates. He had fulfilled his father's instructions and become an advocate after all. Two days later, on July 16th, they called him to the Bar.

He fled from Edinburgh to his cousin, Bob, at the Forest of Fontainebleau, and stayed at Siron's Inn. By September he was back in Edinburgh, practising law. He received four briefs and earned four guineas.

The law did not enchant him, and he preferred to write, but published nothing except some reviews. He was still living on his father, with spending money of £84 a year, at the age of twenty-five. At the end of the year he had six shillings in his possession, but owed money. *The Illustrated London News* published his story of a walking tour in Galloway during 1876, but that could not have made him very much richer. There were also several essays in *Cornhill*. At this time Henley comforted him, and he must have needed comfort, for the situation of a man of twenty-five still dependent on his father, with 30s. a week pocket money and a few guineas made by writing is not enviable. In September came the canoe trip from Antwerp to Pontoise mentioned already, and then he was back at Grez, on the fringe of the Forest of Fontainebleau, once more.

This time there were two women at table where before all had been men, two art-students from California, a Mrs. and Miss Osbourne. Stevenson, arriving by canoe, and, making a dramatic entrance into the dining-room, saw his future wife for the first time.

She was thirty-five, ten years older than he, had been married for nineteen years, and possessed a daughter of seventeen and a son of eight. It was almost inevitable that Stevenson should marry a woman older than himself, because his demand from women had always been that they should mother him: first his own mother, then Mrs. Sitwell, and finally his wife. One might well doubt if, without Fanny Osbourne, born Fanny van der Grift, he would have won fame as a writer. He could have written of her, as Kipling's soldier wrote of his first mistress:

> "*Aggie de Castrer she made me,*
> *An' Aggie was clever as sin;*
> *Older than me, but my first 'un—*
> *More like a mother she were—*
> *Showed me the way to promotion an' pay,*
> *And I learned about women from 'er!*"

Not that he ever learned much about women, for, as a critic has said, "his heroines, where there are any, are mere boys in petticoats, and his subsidiary women characters little more than part of the scenery or background of the action", but the little he did learn, Fanny taught him.

It took a brave woman to marry him, what with his delicate health, his egoism, and his complete lack of money sense, but Fanny had been bred in a hard school and could draw on her nineteen years' experience of one unfortunate marriage. As a person I find her more interesting, and infinitely more attractive, than Stevenson.

She was an American, Dutch on her father's side and Swedish on her mother's. Born in 1840, she spent her childhood in the backwoods around Indianapolis, where the family spun its own clothes and grew its own food. The National Road connected them with the outside world, and Indians lurked in the neighbourhood, so little Fanny van der Grift grew up wild.

In December 1857 she married a twenty-year-old Kentucky youth named Samuel Osbourne. He fought for the North in the Civil War (1861–1865), leaving Fanny and their baby girl. Eventually he told her to join him in California. Upon arriving there she found that he had departed for Nevada to go silver-mining. She continued to Nevada, and for seven years lived in a mining camp where there were only six women.

Her next home was Virginia City, then a mining camp. In the ninth year of her marriage, Samuel left her again, but she joined him in San Francisco. She heard he had been killed by Indians and went into mourning, but one day he arrived safe and sound. They lived at San Francisco, and her son, Lloyd Osbourne, Stevenson's collaborator, was born on April 7th, 1868.

Soon afterwards her husband, who had been unfaithful before, was unfaithful again, and she lived apart from him, but went back and lived with him at Brooklyn. Later she and her daughter studied art at the San Francisco School of Art. She bore a third child, a boy, in 1871, and when he had reached his fourth year she left her husband for good on account of his liaisons with other women. In 1875 she sailed for Europe with her children and studied art in Paris, being at the time desperately poor. The youngest child died in Paris, and so Fanny Osbourne, worn out with unhappiness, departed for Grez, and there Stevenson met her, and they fell in love. Compared with Fanny Osbourne, he was a child in experience, but she loved him deeply.

We now have the picture of Stevenson, aged twenty-five, in delicate health, passionately in love, with no money, anxious to marry a woman ten years older than himself, the mother of a grown-up daughter, and a son, already married to someone else. It is all very Stevensonian.

He returned to Edinburgh to consider the situation, but took no definite step towards marrying Fanny until the year 1879.

The intervening years are somewhat vague and indefinite. At some time, probably in 1876, though no one knows the exact date, he received £1,000 from his father on account of his eventual inheritance. Theoretically, Thomas Stevenson did right in paying over this money, and practically he did wrong, for Stevenson was not to be trusted with money, having no money sense. Any hard-up friend had only to ask him for money and he gave it. When he had none left he appealed to his father for more as a matter of course. By 1877 he had £800 left of his £1,000. Two years later it had all disappeared.

He spent much of the three years which followed his falling in love with Fanny in Paris and at Fontainebleau, though he was in London in 1877; for there he met Edmund Gosse once more, with whom, as we have seen, he became acquainted in Scotland, and made another of his dazzling friendships. That year he did very little writing, but it saw the birth of his first story, entitled *A Lodging for the Night*, which appeared in *Temple Bar*. The scene of the story was Paris in the middle ages.

The beginning of 1878 found him at Dieppe writing *The Inland Voyage*, very hard up. He decided to tell all his troubles to his father, and Thomas Stevenson journeyed to Paris, a little wearily perhaps, for Smout tried him pretty highly, listened sympathetically, and returned to his home in Edinburgh, where the solid house in the solid city must have seemed grateful and comforting after the Latin Quarter of Paris and his wayward son.

In April Stevenson was with his parents at Burford Bridge, in Surrey, where he met George Meredith. In the summer he returned to France, bought a donkey, which he christened "Modestine", for sixty-five francs and set off with Modestine for a walking tour in the Cevennes. The result was his book *Travels with a Donkey in the Cevennes*.

By the end of the year Fanny had returned to California. She was still married to Samuel Osbourne, but on reaching California she decided to divorce him. Meanwhile, she lived with her son and daughter and her youngest sister at Monterey.

As for Stevenson, he was now twenty-eight, and had written in five years twenty-eight essays and five short stories. There were also two books, *An Inland Voyage* and *Picturesque Notes on Edinburgh*. Some of this proved to be his best work, but from the point of view of appreciation he was still a collector's piece. The general public hardly knew of him.

It was in July 1879 that he burned his boats, and against the warning of his friends in London, without consulting his parents, left England for California to join Fanny. As usual, he had hardly any money.

In a farewell letter to a friend, he said that Fanny was ill but that he hoped to be back in a month or two. In one to his father he described his own feelings as of death rather than life. This seems almost prophetic, for in a short time he was to be very near death.

Because he had little money, he sailed in the *Devonia*, an emigrant ship, though he travelled second cabin, for he wanted a table to write on, hoping to keep himself by writing, and Fanny as well if necessary. He wrote home proudly that he had completed thirty pages of a story in ten days at sea—an average of three pages a day, which is not much for a professional writer of fiction.

From New York, where he arrived on August 18th, he travelled by emigrant train to San Francisco. The journey takes several days, and the accommodation on the train did not permit him to lie down. At San Francisco, on August 30th, he heard from Fanny that she was better, and proceeded to try to work his way to her at Monterey. He found a job as a cowboy twenty miles from her, but, having no cowboy experience, lost himself, fell off his horse, and spent three days in the open country.

There an old frontiersman found him, saw he was ill, and took him to his ranch. He reached Monterey, and was nursed by a Frenchman, Jules Simoneau, who kept a café there. But his health never recovered from the emigrant ship, the emigrant train, and the hardships of the journey from San Francisco to Monterey.

He stayed there three months, and Fanny's youngest sister, Nellie van der Grift, afterwards Mrs. Sanchez, who lived with her, has left us a picture of Stevenson and Fanny in those days. Both were ill as they waited for Fanny's divorce to go through. At the beginning of 1880 they were back in San Francisco. As usual, lack of money was the cause of Stevenson's troubles. Fanny obtained her divorce, and her ex-husband, Samuel Osbourne, had promised to keep her till Stevenson married her, but Osbourne lost a Government appointment and his income with it. Stevenson had £40, which he said would last him four months. In that time, surely he could make another £50?

He wrote home passionately to his friends, particularly to Sidney Colvin. He also worked as he had never worked before, with the sole idea of making money. At San Francisco he lived in one room, and allowed himself a fifty-cent (2s. 0d.) dinner and a ten-cent breakfast. His friends at home—Colvin and W. E. Henley—told him his work was deteriorating. He replied that he must make £200 a year, and in the previous year, on account of illness, he had only made £109. This was his ambition in his thirtieth year.

His health broke down, and in March and April he was ill with pleurisy, malaria, and exhaustion. Fanny and the doctor saved him. Above all, his father rescued him, financially, once more.

Thomas Stevenson had felt his son's abrupt departure to the United States so much that at one time he planned to leave Edinburgh for some place where no one knew him. But when he heard that Stevenson was ill and poverty-stricken in California, he let him know that he could have what money he needed. Stevenson wrote to Colvin that he could count on his parents for £250 a year, and that when he returned to Scotland

his wife and he would be welcome guests. Stevenson married
Fanny on May 19th, 1880. It was the best day's work he ever
did. They were both ill, but Stevenson felt a morbid satisfaction in the knowledge that if he died Fanny would be paid
a small pension as the widow of an Edinburgh advocate.

He did not die, and Fanny was to make a man of him.

They did not start married life in a *solitude à deux*, like most
married couples. There were with them Fanny's son, and her
sister. Her daughter was now married. They spent some time
in the California mountains, and then came the moment of
departure for England, and Edinburgh, and Stevenson's
family. Fanny feared the meeting because she feared Thomas
Stevenson, but she liked the sound of her mother-in-law.

At the dock at Liverpool to meet them were Mr. and Mrs.
Stevenson and Sidney Colvin, and so all the family became
united: Thomas Stevenson aged sixty-two, his wife aged fifty-
one, Fanny aged forty, and Robert Louis Stevenson, the baby
of the party, aged twenty-nine. The year was 1880. There was
also Fanny's son; her sister remained in California.

Fanny's fears evaporated, and she and Thomas Stevenson
became great friends, but her stay in Scotland lasted only a
few months. Stevenson was now almost a physical wreck,
suffering from lung disease, acute catarrh, and great weakness.
His doctor insisted that he must spend each winter at Davos,
and there he went with Fanny and her son. He had permission
to write a little, and produced a few essays and poems, but his
weakness prevented a great deal of work.

Fanny had already begun her life of devotion. The altitude
of Davos made her ill, but she did not complain. She was
surrounded by invalids at Davos, and the contrast with the
gaiety of California, laughing in the sun, depressed her, but
she could not fight against destiny. For her husband it was a
choice between Davos and death.

In April 1881 they left Davos for Barbizon, staying at Siron's
establishment, as of old. The summer they spent in Scotland.
At Pitlochry Stevenson wrote *Thrawn Janet*, *The Merry Men*,
and *The Body Snatchers*, and Fanny helped with them all. In
August they moved to Braemar, and there Stevenson began
A Child's Garden of Verses and *Treasure Island*. In the autumn it
was a case of Davos once more.

Poor Fanny! She became very ill, and had to go down to Berne to see specialists. Stevenson remained behind; for him it was altitude or nothing. He complained to a friend "how rotten he was feeling", alone with a German maid in a châlet on top of a hill. Fanny did not recover till the following February. That winter he finished *Treasure Island,* most of *The Silverado Squatters,* and some essays. *Treasure Island* was serialised in *Little Folks,* the price being £2 10s., a page for serial use.

In May 1882 Fanny was able to put Davos behind her for good; the doctor said Stevenson need not return here, and could live in France. The summer passed in Scotland, and in September Stevenson had a haemorrhage—not his first. Accordingly he and his cousin, R.A.M. ("Bob"), went to France to find a home, and settled, after Fanny had followed him, in a house near Marseilles, where they spent ten weeks, with Stevenson continuing his haemorrhages, and then left for Nice, taking eventually a châlet at Hyères. Here they engaged Valentine Roch as a maid, a treasure who stayed with them for six years.

That year (1883) he made, for the first time, more than £300; but he was often in debt, and had to pay for Lloyd Osbourne's, his stepson's, education. Still, in financial crises, his father never failed him. At the end of 1883 he could tell his parents that he had £50 left, no bills, £100 due in a week, and £150 in a month. In the past year he had earned £495 0s. 6d.

In January 1884 he was so ill that the doctor gave up hope of his life. He recovered, but by April he had fallen ill again, his illness being complicated by eye trouble; he could not walk, he could not read, he was forbidden to speak, and he said:

"If this goes on I shall soon have nothing to eat."

In May he suffered the worst haemorrhage of them all, and once more nearly died; it was during this severe illness that he wrote his poem "Requiem" which begins:

> "*Under the wide and starry sky,*
> *Dig the grave and let me lie.*
> *Glad did I live and gladly die,*
> *And I laid me down with a will.*"

He was back in England by July 1st, staying first at Richmond and then at Bournemouth, where Sargent painted his portrait. His health remained so good at Bournemouth throughout the winter that in the new year the faithful Thomas Stevenson bought a house there which he gave to Fanny. Stevenson christened it "Skerryvore". There he remained, an invalid it is true, for three years.

I have given the story of Stevenson's early married life in some detail in order to show how much Fanny had to put up with. She found herself tied to a chronic invalid, all her time taken up with the business of nursing him. She never faltered, and all Stevenson's best work was done after his marriage. If he had died before he married Fanny little would have been heard of him. Yet at Bournemouth frequently she was ill herself, but still she nursed him devotedly, and acted constructively in his working life as the critic on the hearth.

A Child's Garden of Verses appeared in 1885, and in that year also Stevenson completed his first successful book from the point of view of the general public: *The Strange Case of Dr. Jekyll and Mr. Hyde.* The story came to him in a dream, and Fanny awakened him from it because he screamed in his sleep. This book made him famous among readers both in England and the United States, and also added an expression to the English language.

He had now nine more years to live, but they were to be the most dramatic years of his life. He paid his last visit to Paris, the city which had given him Fanny, in the summer of 1886; during the winter he was ill again at Bournemouth, and his parents took a house there to be near him. In the spring they returned to Edinburgh because Thomas Stevenson's health was failing. He died on May 8th, 1887, and though Stevenson travelled with his wife to Scotland he arrived too late for his father to recognise him.

No one will ever know what Thomas Stevenson thought of his son in his heart of hearts, but in all the many crises of Stevenson's life he had stood by to offer a helping hand, and the credit for Stevenson's achievement is as much his, and Fanny's, as Stevenson's.

He was too ill to attend his father's funeral, and when he left Edinburgh for Bournemouth he had looked his last on his native city. With the death of his father he felt that the ties which bound him to Britain had been cut, and he might have remarked with Tennyson:

> "*Yet waft me from the harbour mouth,*
> *Wild wind; I seek a warmer sky,*
> *And I shall see before I die*
> *The palms and temples of the South.*"

He had dreamed of the Pacific ever since that far-off talk with J. Seed, once Secretary to the Customs and Marine Department of New Zealand, in 1874. Now arrived the opportunity to make the dream come true. It was evident that he could never expect tolerable health unless he emigrated to a warm and equable climate. Therefore he arranged with his mother, his father's inheritrix, now fifty-eight, to leave Edinburgh and travel to the United States with Fanny and himself. Beyond the United States his plans were still vague. They sailed on August 22nd, 1887, from London, in a ship with the unromantic name of *Ludgate Hill*, accompanied by the faithful Valentine Roch whom they had engaged at Hyères, and Sidney Colvin saw them off. It was his last sight of Stevenson, who, without knowing it, was leaving England for ever.

He had behind him *Treasure Island*, *The Strange Case of Dr. Jekyll and Mr. Hyde* and *Kidnapped*, and his reputation as a writer stood high in the United States.

The *Ludgate Hill* was a cattle ship, and also carried monkeys, but he enjoyed the voyage. The editor of *Scribner's Magazine*, who was to put much money in his way, met him on the New York dockside. As soon as he had settled in New York, other important editors flocked to greet him. He found himself lionised as only Americans lionise a distinguished literary man.

By October Stevenson craved for the sea once more, and his mother, now a wealthy woman, offered to charter a yacht. However, it was decided that Stevenson should go to a sanatorium for consumptives at Saranac. There Mr. McClure, the famous American editor, called to offer him $10,000 a year (about £2,000) for a weekly essay in the *New York World*. He also offered to syndicate *The Black Arrow* as a serial.

Scribner's Magazine offered £700 for twelve articles. The United States seemed to be paved with gold.

But the dream of the Pacific held, and McClure promised that if Stevenson would cruise in the Pacific and write travel articles they should be syndicated for enough money to pay for the cruise.

In 1888 the dream came true. The winter at Saranac had improved Stevenson's health, so that he spent some time in New York and at Manasquam on the coast of New Jersey. But Fanny was in San Francisco looking over yachts, and finally settled on one, the *Casco*, a seventy-ton fore-and-aft topsail schooner. She was a luxury yacht owned by a millionaire. Stevenson did not hesitate about the charter, and wrote to England for £2,000 of the £3,000 he had inherited from his father.

He boarded the *Casco* on June 26th, 1888, and sailed two days later; the crew were the captain, three Swedes, one Finn and one Chinese; the passengers Stevenson, his wife and mother, Lloyd Osbourne and Valentine Roch. Mrs. Stevenson was a good sailor; Fanny feared and hated the sea, but she acquiesced because her husband and son loved it.

They steered for the Marquesas Islands, and in a month anchored off Nukahiva, remained three weeks, and got on well with the natives, one-time cannibals; cruised through the Low Archipelago, and reached the Society Islands in October. There two things happened; Stevenson developed haemorrhage again, and met Princess Moë, a native royalty, who called to enquire after his health, and made him a raw fish salad with her own royal hands; rather in the manner of Queen Elizabeth feeding the dying Burghley with pottage. Fortunately the parallel was not exact; Stevenson was not dying.

There the captain punched the mast in a fit of temper, his fist sank into it, and it was discovered to be full of dry rot. They sent the *Casco* to Papeete for repairs, and the party remained at Tautira. There was feasting, and Stevenson became a brother of the sub-chief by the simple ceremony of exchanging names.

Then tragedy befell. The *Casco* did not come back. The party ran out of stores and money. The sub-chief "brother" solved the problem. They were to be his guests till the *Casco* arrived. Stevenson settled down to work on *The Master of Ballantrae*. The *Casco* returned and they left on Christmas Day for Honolulu. There Stevenson found everything in his mail but money. But he made friends with King Kalakaua, who then ruled in those parts, and finished *The Master of Ballantrae*.

By May Mrs. Stevenson seems to have had enough of the wilds, since she left for Scotland. Her son, his money difficulties over, chartered the sixty-two-ton *Equator*, and decided not to return to England for another year. Valentine Roch also had had enough of sailing, so the only passengers were Stevenson, Fanny, and her son. King Kalakaua said good-bye with musicians and champagne, and the Stevensons disappeared into the blue for six months.

Having decided to sail for the Gilbert Islands, Stevenson changed his mind, for the idea of *The Wrecker* had occurred to him, and he proposed to write it, mail it from Samoa, and then start on a trading cruise. By December 1889 they were back at Samoa once more.

They stayed at Apia, the capital of the Island of Upolu, for six weeks and then Stevenson, delighted with the Island, bought three hundred acres of land on a mountainside where he meant to build a home and live when he was not at sea. The site, and the ever-changing plans of Stevenson, recall Ralph Hodgson's verse:

> " *The final Dodo gathered wool*
> *Upon a mountain side;*
> *His energy was wonderful,*
> *And, finally, he died.*"

Stevenson had planned also to reach England by June 1890, but it was not to be. He sailed for Sydney, in a steamer this time, with Fanny, in February 1890, and at Sydney fell seriously ill once more. Consequently he and Fanny and her son sailed in another steamer for the Gilbert Islands, and he arranged to reach England by September. Unfortunately his health did not improve at sea, though the voyage lasted four months.

They were at Sydney again in August, and once more his health failed. It was then that he gave up the prospect of going home, arranged for his furniture to be sent out from England, and returned to Apia, for good.

In Apia he became almost a legendary figure, a patriarch in the home, the uncrowned king of the Island. It was a picturesque state which appealed to him.

First they had a four-roomed house, but on his estate, which he called Vailima, six hundred feet above sea level, he built the house of his dreams. Fanny had seen enough pioneering in her youth not to feel dismayed by the enterprise of clearing ground and building. There were all kinds of set-backs and misfortunes, and the business of housekeeping would have driven anyone but an experienced pioneer crazy. Stevenson's mother appeared in January 1891, in the midst of the confusion whilst they still had only the four-roomed house. She had come to live there for good since her son would never return to England. However, seeing what the conditions were, she returned to Sydney for some months until building should be finished.

At the end of May they had their house, a wooden house, with a roof of corrugated iron—the "curse of the tropics"— and the house-warming took place in the summer, with Stevenson, Fanny, his mother, his stepson Lloyd Osbourne, and Fanny's married daughter, Mrs. Strong, with her small boy. In the end all their servants were Samoans, and Stevenson became head of a household of five white people and twelve native servants. He read family prayers in the great hall.

Though now prosperous, he ran true to form over money. In 1892 he extended his house, and found himself spending all he earned. Still, the house looked imposing, with two verandas, one on each floor.

He missed his friends in England, particularly Sidney Colvin, and tried to persuade them to visit him, but he was too distant and none came.

The Samoan War broke out in the spring of 1893, and Stevenson, reluctantly, could not intervene, though, as he pointed out, he need only ride nine miles to be created a general. He occupied himself with hospital work, and by September the war ended. After the war he visited Honolulu and became very ill there, so that he could not return to

Vailima till November. In the New Year of 1894, his last year on earth, arrangements had been completed for the Edinburgh Edition of his writings, a complete edition, and this gave him great joy.

He needed comfort because he became obsessed with the writer's greatest fear, that he has written himself out. He now wrote with difficulty, and the effort exhausted him; and having always lived up to his income he began to wonder what would happen if the power of writing left him altogether. His money worries were groundless, for he died a rich man, but he could never understand money, and never knew accurately his financial position.

His friends in England cabled to him that the Edinburgh Edition would make him richer by from £6,000 to £8,000, but he never seems to have grasped the fact that he had no need to worry about money.

Very near the end of his journey the ease of writing returned, and he worked light-heartedly on *Weir of Hermiston* which he was destined never to finish. He set his scene in Edinburgh, and he might have quoted A. E. Housman, if the lines had already been published:

> "*Into my heart an air that kills*
> *From your far country blows:*
> *What are those blue remembered hills,*
> *What spires, what farms are those?*
>
> *That is the land of lost content,*
> *I see it shining plain,*
> *The happy highways where I went*
> *And cannot come again.*"

On December 3rd, 1894, he had been working on *Weir of Hermiston*. Fanny was feeling depressed, and so for dinner he brought out a bottle of good Burgundy. Suddenly he asked: "Do I look strange?" and fell to the ground. He had had a cerebral haemorrhage.

They carried him, unconscious, to the great hall. Two doctors arrived, a clergyman knelt and prayed, but the dying man remained unconscious to the end.

The Samoans cut a path up the mountain, dug the grave on the peak, and carried the coffin to the grave.

His mother returned to Scotland and lived three years more. Fanny survived till 1914, and died in California. She asked that she might be cremated, and her ashes buried beside her husband.

The Samoans called Stevenson "Tusitala", which means "the teller of tales", and that description fits him best. He was essentially a storyteller, and a boyish storyteller at that. Less than a month before he died, perhaps with a foreboding of death, he said of himself:

"After all, a few tales for boys is about the sum of my achievements." There is a good deal in this half-truth; perhaps the fact that his fame in the United States, a young country, was greater than in more sophisticated England emphasises the boyish note in his work. He never really grew up. For example, his friend, Andrew Lang, met him once in Bond Street. Stevenson, then twenty-three, wore a black shirt, a red tie, what is described as "a black brigand coat" and a velvet smoking cap. No wonder Andrew Lang, who was inclined to be dandified, exclaimed:

"Go away, Louis. My character will stand a great deal, but it won't stand being seen talking to a thing like you in Bond Street."

It is perhaps significant that *Treasure Island* was serialised in *Little Folks*, a magazine for children.

The boyishness is apparent in his fiction. As for Stevenson, the essayist, I cannot help feeling that Lytton Strachey's *Eminent Victorians* and *Portraits in Miniature* are to be preferred to Stevenson's *Familiar Studies of Men and Books*.

"In verse," wrote J. W. Mackail, "Stevenson was only a brilliant amateur; but his poems have all the curious fascination that attaches to the work of a trained artist who diverges for his own amusement into an alien though cognate art."

The same authority concluded:

"In some respects he is an interesting parallel to William Hazlitt, a writer whom, both in substance and in manner, he took in youth for one of his chief models. If to Hazlitt may be applied the caustic saying of Voltaire, 'Sa reputation s'affermira toujours, parce qu'on le lit guère' ('His reputation will always become strengthened because one hardly ever reads him'), so more than half of the various and unequal work that fills the long shelf of Stevenson's collected works will probably become the possession of a small circle of men of letters and be disregarded or forgotten by the wider public."

Stevenson's most fascinating trait was that he did so enjoy himself, and did so enjoy writing what he wrote, except when he was writing for the pot. If fate had been kind he would have been born in the eighteenth century with a stately income, when he might have become a less imposing Horace Walpole.

He owed much to Fanny and his father.

BIBLIOGRAPHY

Chambers' Encyclopaedia of English Literature.
CROSS, J. W. *Life of George Eliot* (3 vols.).
Dictionary of National Biography.
ELLIS, S. M. *George Meredith.*
ELWES, SIMON. *Marian.*
Encyclopaedia Britannica.
FORSTER, JOHN. *Life of Dickens* (3 vols.).
HAMMERTON, J. A. *George Meredith in Anecdote and Criticism.*
ILCHESTER, LORD (Edited by). *Elizabeth Lady Holland to her Son.*
MASSON, ROSALINE. *The Life of Robert Louis Stevenson.*
    ,,   ,, (Edited by): *I Remember Robert Louis Stevenson.*
MELVILLE, LEWIS. *William Makepeace Thackeray* (2 vols.).
New Age Encyclopaedia.
POPE-HENNESSEY, UNA. *Charles Dickens.*
RITCHIE, LADY. *Chapters from some Memoirs.*
    ,,   ,, *Introduction to the Centenary Edition of Thackeray's Works.*
ROSS, JANET ANN. *The Fourth Generation.*
STEBBINS, LUCY POATE and RICHARD POATE. *The Trollopes.*
STEVENSON, ROBERT LOUIS (Edited by SIDNEY COLVIN). *Letters to his Family and Friends.*
Times Literary Supplement.
TROLLOPE, ANTHONY. *An Autobiography.*
VIZETELLY, HENRY. *Glances Back Through Seventy Years.*